The Prolific Knitting Machine

The
Prolific
Knitting Machine

by
Catherine Cartwright-Jones

*To my husband, who taught this Luddite to knit
and use a word processor; to Rhys and Gwyneddh;
and to my mother, who listened*

Illustrations by Catherine Cartwright-Jones
Typesetting by Marc Owens
Back cover photo by Ann Swider Photography,
Cleveland Heights, Ohio

Interweave Press
201 East Fourth Street
Loveland, Colorado 80537

Library of Congress Catalog Number
ISBN 0-934026-58-0
First printing: 7.5M:91390:PP/CL

Library of Congress Cataloging in Publication Data
Cartwright-Jones, Catherine, 1950–
    The prolific knitting machine / by Catherine Cartwright
    Jones.
        p.   cm.
    Includes index.
    ISBN 0-934026-58-0 : $17.95
    1. Knitting, Machine.   2. Knit goods.   3. Sewing
    I. Title.
TT680.C435   1990
746.9'2--dc20
                                      90-4592
                                      CIP

Contents

What's this book good for, anyway?

Why do so many sweaters languish unfinished, unloved, and unworn? It's hard to get one to come out right! There are some nasty obstacles between lovely skeins of yarn in your arms and a lovely sweater on your back.

Every yarn in the shop knits up differently. You just don't know how they'll look until you try them.

Your knitting machine is unique. It has quirks that only you have noticed. If your machine is a complex one, it can have a personality of its own, complete with talents, neurotic behavior, and the occasional burst of temper. It does not knit at precisely the same gauge as its twin from the factory. In addition, you handle your machine in a particular way, and you will get a slightly different gauge from it than another knitter would.

Can you find a pattern in just your size? Sizes are standardized; people are not. Bodies come in a vast and magnificent array, not S, M, and L. Can you find a design that suits your taste, your personality, and your needs? Or would you rather knit the beautiful, and perfectly suitable, sweaters that currently reside in your imagination?

And even if you could find the perfect pattern in your size, and the perfect yarn, which would work for your machine at the correct gauge . . . would you still be flummoxed by the instructions, which seem to be written in Martian?

There's a cure for all these problems. Design and draft your own sweaters. I plan and make about 250 sweaters a year for people. All of these sweaters are one-of-a-kind, and all of the people are one-of-a-kind. I'll tell you what I do to get the job done.

I figure out what gauge my yarn makes on my machine. I take measurements of the people and draft a pattern. I use a few shortcuts that eliminate the tedious bits, and I know a few other tricks to make the sweaters look like pricey boutique wonders rather than church bazaar bargains. I let the knitting machine do what it does best—make fabric—and I do the shaping with the help of a sewing machine, in a technique called *half-fashioning*. It's simple, and it works.

Soon you'll be able to knit your ideas quickly and have them fit perfectly, so you can move on to the important business of wearing them. Here's how.

All the Technical Bits

or, how to get it made and looking good

Equipment

You will need some basic equipment to design, draft, and knit your ideas—but you've probably already got it all. You will also need some technical garment-making skills—simple stuff, but it works like hocus-pocus to turn yarn into a sweater, magically instead of miserably.

First, assemble the following:

a *knitting machine* of any sort, but preferably with a ribber*

a *sewing machine* that will reliably produce a straight stitch and a zigzag

a *calculator,* or a good head for arithmetic

a *tape measure*

long pins; those used for quilting are especially good

a *washing machine* that has a spin cycle

a *dryer,* if you will work with cotton or acrylic yarns

a *box of kids' chalk*

sharp (SHARP!) *sewing scissors*

a *steam iron,* ideally the kind that snorts steam when you press a button

a big, sturdy *ironing board;* try an old one!

I am not going to tell you how to use your knitting machine. Its manufacturer and dealer should have done that for you, and I hope you and your machine are fairly well acquainted. If basic knitting on your machine leaves you raging and brimming with tears, you need to go see the person who sold it to you. If you can knit straight rows without the knitting's landing on the floor *too* often, but feel competent to make only baby blankets, then this is your book.

I'll concentrate on technical information which I haven't seen in other books, and which I find essential to happy machine knitting. Knitting machines are supposed to make lovely garments, not make good people weep.

*See page 65 if you don't have a ribber.

Choosing yarn

A few simple guidelines for choosing yarns will save you hours of grief and give you control over what you knit. You will be drafting your own patterns from your own gauge, and the fit of your garments will depend on the accuracy of your gauge calculations. If you get them correct for one garment, it will be more convenient and reliable to use the same yarn for several garments.

Every yarn has a personality, and the more often you work with a yarn, the finer will be your rapport with it. Each yarn has slightly different requirements for knitting, sewing, finishing, and laundering. If you know your yarn as well as an old friend, brilliant results will be customary, not happenstance.

You know a few yarns that your knitting machine glides through beautifully, and a few that

give it fits. Most knitting machines, especially those of the standard (rather than bulky) variety, prefer smooth yarns to the nubbly and hairy. Simple yarns are also more predictable for laundering and wearing. I look for smooth, natural-fiber yarns that a mill is producing in a wide array of colors. Once I've found a yarn I love, I make dozens of sweaters from it.

Knitting a sweater is enough of a challenge when you *can* predict your yarn's and your machine's personality crises. Beware of enticing, enchanting yarns which may be vicious to knit with, and may inflict serious damage on your helpless machine. You can have plenty of fun and make lots of gorgeous sweaters without making your life miserable.

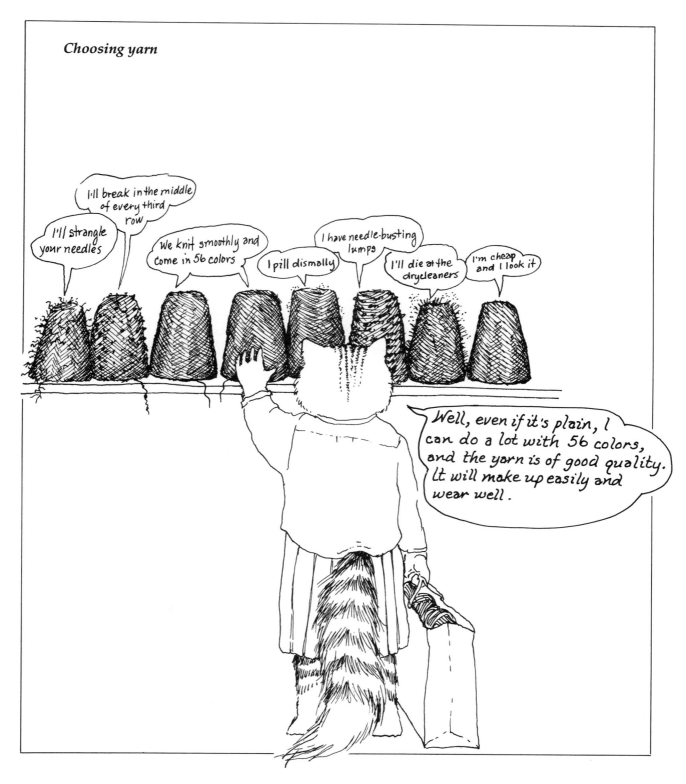

Make small test swatches

Try different yarns,
different tensions,
different fulling—
find out what works.

Calculating your gauge

When you have found a couple of yarns you think you can work and live with well, knit some small swatches at different gauges. Then full these, according to the fulling instructions on the next page.

Handle the swatches, fiddle with them, rub them against your cheek, pin them up on the wall, live with them for a few days. Then decide which should make the best garment.

Next, knit a large swatch of your favorite combination. If your garment will have ribbing, include enough rows so you can figure a gauge for ribbing as well as knitting. Full the completed swatch (see page 15). If this seems like a great waste of time

and materials, consider that if you don't have enough information to draft your garment accurately and finish it well, you will be in the middle of a very expensive waste, indeed.

Press your fulled large swatch and measure it. Divide stitches by inches. Divide rows by inches. Use a calculator, and round off at one decimal place. If your gauge is 9.624 rows per inch, for example, round off to 9.6, not 10, rows per inch. Inaccuracies make gorgeous sweaters ill-fitting and unwearable.

For each new yarn you acquire, you *must* go through this process.

Make a large gauge swatch

I make square swatches to try out yarns. I'll sew them up to make an afghan.

I make wide swatches and sew them into caps when I'm done.

I make extra large swatches and sew them up as pillows; I stuff the pillows with waste yarn and blunders.

*Once you have a fabric you like,
accurate gauge information
comes from BIG swatches*

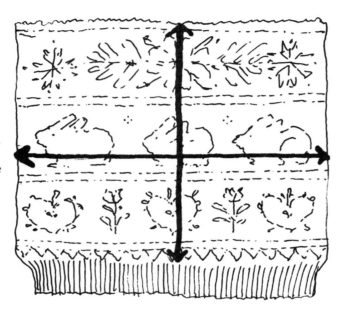

You'll need accurate gauge figures, so knit a sample at least 7" by 7", including a sample of ribbing if your machine can rib.

Count how many stitches are in the width of the swatch, and how many rows are in the non-ribbing area. Measure side to side, and top to ribbing.

Number of stitches wide _____ ÷ number of inches wide _____ = **stitches per inch.**

Number of rows long _____ ÷ number of inches long _____ = **rows per inch.**

| **Gauge** |
| _____ stitches/inch |
| _____ rows/inch |

You may as well use a calculator; this won't come out even. Round off to one or two decimal places — don't round off to the even number.

Fulling

Fulling is the fine, old process of getting a freshly knitted or woven bit of cloth to stop looking uneasy and recalcitrant, and to make it relaxed, supple, and soft. Most things which have been rammed through 200 hookety needles a few hundred times will become edgy and stiff. Your yarn was very much startled by being knitted and needs some Tender Loving Care to settle down and be a good-looking sweater.

Fulling wool. When you have knitted all the necessary pieces and trimmed the dangling yarns to 2" at the selvedges, put the collection of fabric in a sink or bathtub or washing machine full of cool water. You may want to prepare the cool water first. If you add hair conditioner the wool will end up glossier and softer. A little shampoo or dishwashing liquid will make the fabric denser, if you want that, and will also remove any streaks of knitting machine grease. These additional substances should be mixed into the water but not poured directly onto the wool.

Let the wool soak for 3 minutes, until it is very soggy, and then agitate—gently or not at all—for less than 1 minute. The more wool is agitated, soaped, or heated, the more it will resemble felt.

Drain the lot. Drop the soggy heap into the washing machine and put on the spin cycle. When the water has been flung out, lay all the pieces flat on towels or a wooden drying rack.

Fulling cotton. Hand-repair all dropped stitches, holes, and blunders. Use a sewing machine to zig-zag across any raw edges, or the knitting will unravel. Clip all the loose ends to 2". Then put the knitted pieces into a washing machine set for a short wash cycle and cold water.

Then shift the whole lot to a dryer on hot, and tumble dry until the fabric is as dry as popcorn. Cotton fulls and shrinks vastly in the dryer, and will appear *very* different after this treatment. Do not panic if your work looks like a mess.

Heat up your iron and get out the spray starch (it's available in a non-aerosol pump sprayer). Press the knitting with lots of steam and a little starch and it will look terrific.

Fulling silk. Don't wash the silk; though silk can be washed, the dyes often run and silk knits become unmanageably heavy with water and slump out of shape. Because silk does not "fluff" when washed, it won't be improved by a soaking. So when you have finished all the pieces, just pull on each one lengthwise to firm up the stitches, then iron them thoroughly with plenty of steam and spray starch.

Fulling other fibers. Read the manufacturer's instructions for fiber care and try them on a swatch. Experiment with a few methods selected from the ideas above. See which swatch comes out most to your liking.

Stitch gouges are fine for measuring gerbils, but misleading and inaccurate for knitting.

The tools manufactured for figuring knitting gauges assume that you can get precise gauge numbers from a very small piece of fabric.

Measuring

Humankind comes in such a rainbow of shapes that commercial sizes are a bad joke to most of us. A sweater can be made to fit anyone; no body is more difficult than any other. A tape measure recognizes no perfect size 10. A toddler, a linebacker, an amputee, a ballerina, a lady wrestler, a jockey, and a great grandmother are all one to a tape measure.

Which measurements you take aren't much different from one person to the next. You'll know if you need some extra measurements: your collars always seem tight, wrist cuffs always gap, or everything binds under the armpits or rides up over a pillowy bit. Measure extra where discomfort has been experienced. When you draft the sweater, the extra measurements will tell you what to do. If

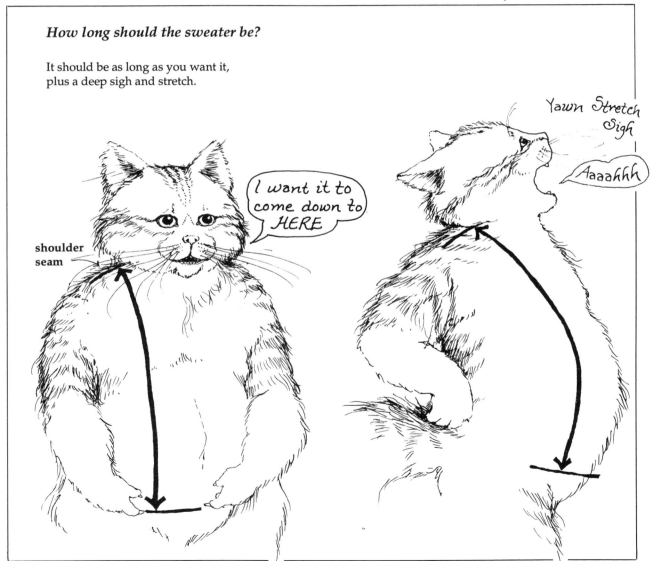

How long should the sweater be?

It should be as long as you want it,
plus a deep sigh and stretch.

your body or your needs are extraordinary—if you need a sweater 3" longer in the back for horseback riding, or you need to accommodate a few missing bits, prostheses, or two vast, iridescent wings—you are the one person in the world who is an expert on what you need. Ask yourself!

How long should your sweater be? As long as you want it. Measure length with a deep stretch and sigh, or you'll have to tug and smooth your sweater down every time you reach for something. If you blouse your sweater over a fold, add length for that.

How big around are you? Wear the clothes you'll have on under the sweater, and measure when you are full and comfy. If you're making a sweater that will be thigh-length, take low derrière and thigh measurements.

Arm length extends from the nape of your neck to the bottom of your wrist. The nape is where the garment tags are.

Beyond that, use your own plentiful good sense.

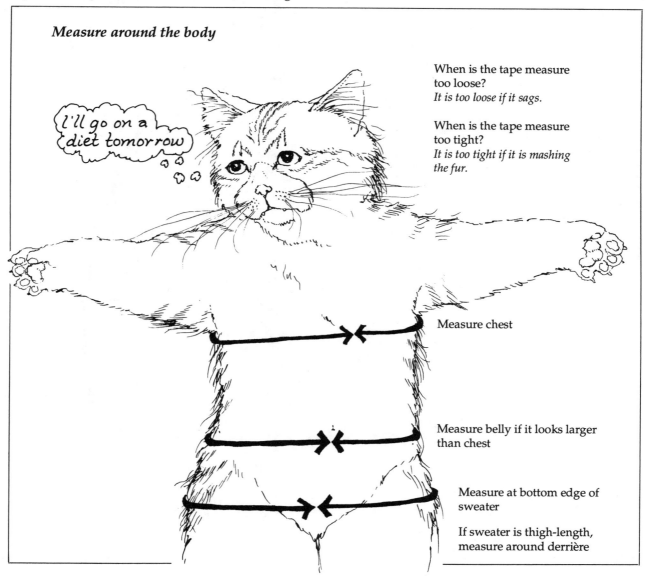

Measure around the body

I'll go on a diet tomorrow

When is the tape measure too loose?
It is too loose if it sags.

When is the tape measure too tight?
It is too tight if it is mashing the fur.

Measure chest

Measure belly if it looks larger than chest

Measure at bottom edge of sweater

If sweater is thigh-length, measure around derrière

17

Measure arm length

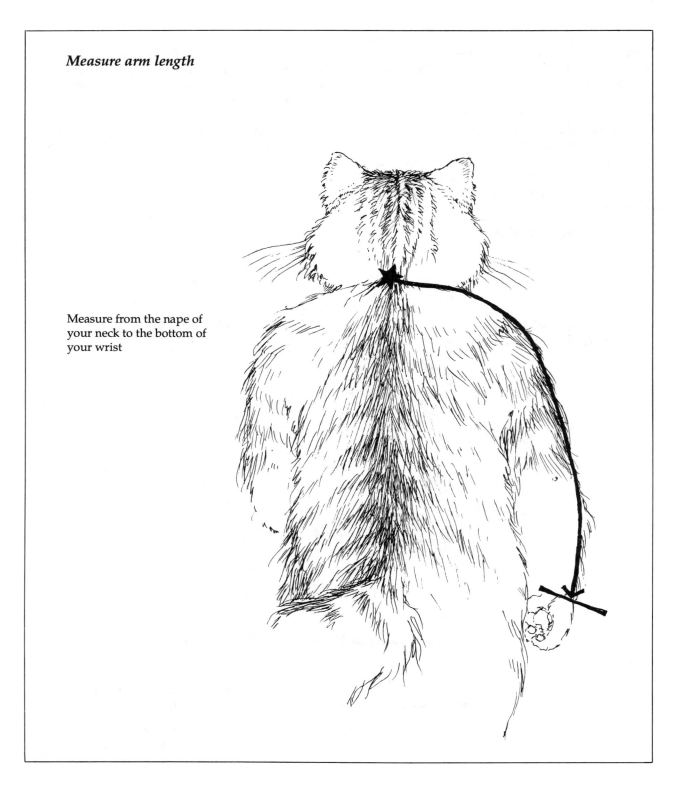

Measure from the nape of
your neck to the bottom of
your wrist

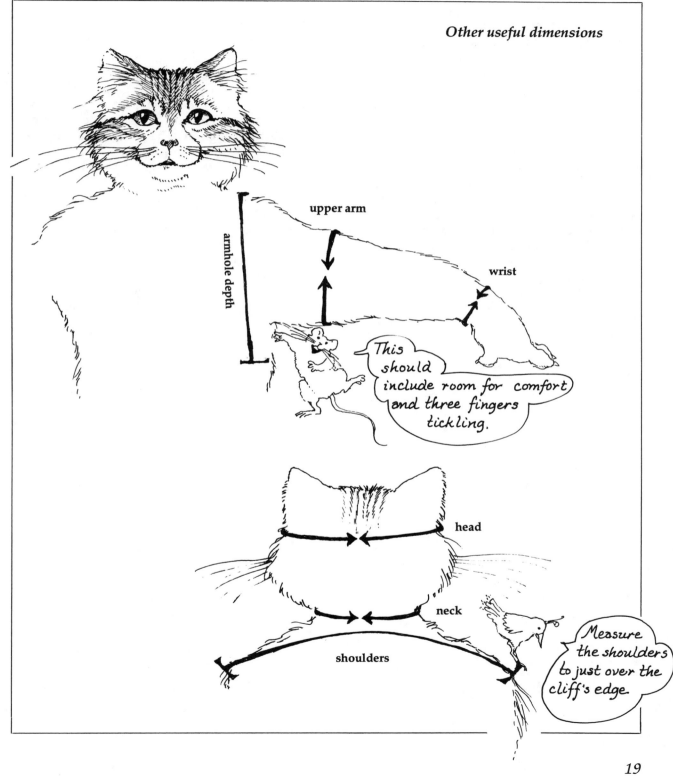

The store-bought sweater, and the value of half-fashioning

A full-fashioned knitted garment is knitted to shape. There are no cut edges, as there would be in a garment of woven cloth. Full-fashioned garments are greatly esteemed because they look tidy on the inside. Historically, when garments have been made of handspun yarn, knitters have not wanted to waste a precious inch of yarn by cutting. (There were also legends of the three Fates, the third of whom ended a human life when she cut the spinner's and weaver's yarn with her shears.) Hand knitters also don't want to make any unnecessary stitches; shaping the garment saves some knitting time, and even unsuperstitious knitters have preferred not to take fatal chances with their garments by cutting threads.

Knitting machines, however, are at their most useful when knitting rectangles and trapezoids. Casting off, shaping neckholes, and tapering shoulderlines are royal nuisances on a knitting machine. Calculating the shaping is difficult, and if anything goes wrong with the gauge the garment will be badly off-size and unfixable.

Therefore, why not use your knitting machine to make the basic shapes for your garment and leave the fine shaping to your chalk, tape measure, sewing machine, and scissors? This method also protects against gauge error, because you can remeasure each piece before sewing. If you discover an error, you can unravel—or rehang and knit a little more.

Half-fashioned garments are not immaculate on the inside. But they don't unravel, the seams are very firm, and they look good on the outside. If you are not planning to enter your sweater in the county fair, and you don't wear your clothes inside out so everyone can admire the exquisite technique, you may as well save yourself several hours of tedious work and a lot of arithmetic. Go ahead and make a half-fashioned sweater.

Half-fashioning is a way to make your home sewing machine do what big sweater companies do with industrial overlock machines. If you have a sturdy overlock machine and know how to use it, terrific! This part you can breeze through. Otherwise, make sure your straight stitch and zigzag are working, and that the teeth that pull the cloth along under the needle aren't worn down.

Half-fashioned seams and steam-finishing

Turn a store-bought sweater inside out. The seams were done on an industrial overlock machine (also known as a serger), unless you have a very expensive sweater there. The good qualities of overlocked seams are that they are narrow and flexible, they don't pucker or stretch the knitted fabric, and they are fast to do. The manufacturer loves overlockers because they save labor costs.

The disadvantage of overlocked seams is that they don't catch all the threads very well! You may find your sweater unraveling at the shoulder or neckline, and when the seams go astray or come loose, they do so in a grand manner.

I use a sturdy, old, home sewing machine to imitate the best qualities of the overlock machines, and avoid the problems. The machine does its job very well on more than 200 sweaters every year.

If you have an overlock machine that handles your knitting well, for heaven's sake, use it. The fine points of this section will be most useful to folks who have a machine capable of zigzag and straight stitches.

Keep looking at that store-bought sweater. The shoulder seam was cut to shape, rather than cast

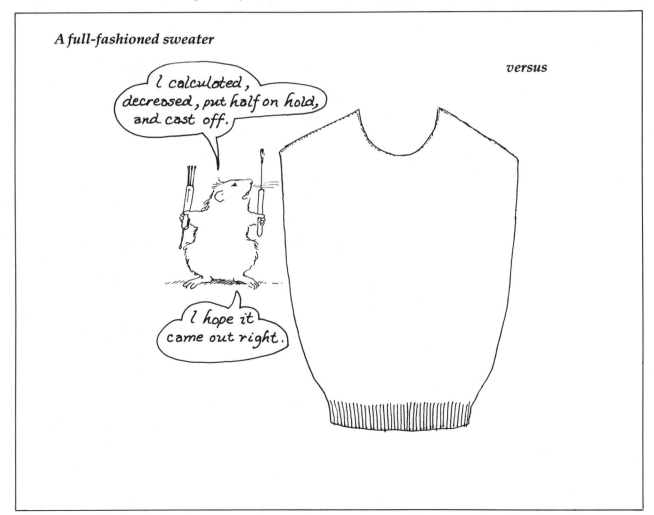

A full-fashioned sweater

versus

I calculated, decreased, put half on hold, and cast off.

I hope it came out right.

off. Raveling was prevented by the zigzag part of the overlock stitch. You can imitate that seam by chalking in the seam line, zigzagging along the line, and sewing the seam itself with a straight stitch just inside the zigzagging. Then you trim off the waste fabric just above the zigzag. The edge may be a tad fuzzy, but it won't unravel. If the fuzz bothers you, get your scissors sharpened. If the thought of wasting bits of yarn is a problem for you, save the scraps to stuff cushions.

The other advantage which that store-bought sweater has is a professional pressing job. Copious steam performs miracles on otherwise waddy-looking lumps of sweater. Get your hands on an iron that blasts out a spray of steam at the punch of a button. A spray bottle which mists clouds upon your ironing is almost as effective. Cotton and silk knitting improves vastly with a generous mist of spray starch.

Make sure you have a big, sturdy ironing board to support all this fuming. A good pressing job is the difference between "You made that yourself?" (derisive snicker) and "You made that yourself?" (envious astonishment).

If you have reason to believe your yarn will die a horrible death if you iron it, try out the effects of fulling and pressing on your test swatch first. Every yarn I've used has responded wonderfully to pressing, but I haven't used every yarn made.

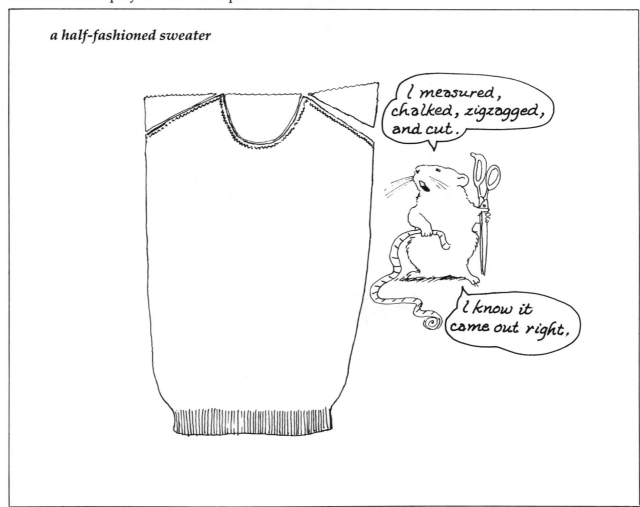

a half-fashioned sweater

Full-fashioned

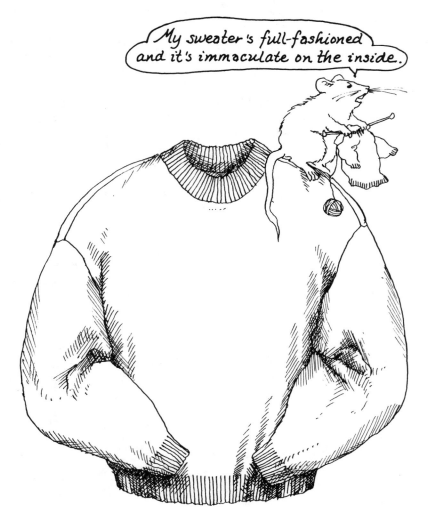

Time involved: much, due to casting off and such
Outside: neat and tidy
Inside: neat and tidy
Likelihood of error: great; errors difficult to fix

Half-fashioned

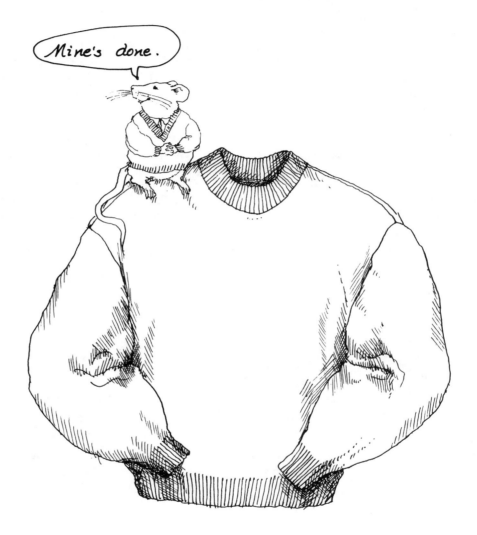

Time involved: half the time—no casting off
Outside: neat and tidy
Inside: a few fuzzy edges, like on store sweaters
Likelihood of error: low, because of easy arithmetic;
   errors easy to fix

Grafting

How can you put two pieces of knitting to-gether? You can either sew a seam, or you can graft. Each technique has its place. A seam is quick, and it shows. A graft is a slow, careful bit of needle-work that is invisible. If you do a careful graft, two bits of knitting will look like one. Use a graft when a seam would look awful.

A graft is useful when you've got fingers to put on gloves, sleeves to shorten, binding to connect, or some unexpected and horrid blunder that must be repaired invisibly so you can avoid reknitting the whole garment.

Look at a piece of knitting that has one row of different-colored knitting in between the other rows. Get out your glasses and stare at it until you think you can make a needle and yarn do what that row is doing—making a row of knitting by earthworming back and forth through the rows above and below it.

Press two bits of knitting that need to be grafted. This will set all the little loops into their shapes and make them less likely to squirm and unravel as you sew through them. Carefully unravel both pieces back to the row you're going to invent with your needle. Thread up a darning needle with the knitting yarn. Move the needle through the loops of the two pieces of knitting, a stitch at a time, pre-cisely imitating a row of knitting.

Be careful to match the tension of your sewing to the tension of the knitting. Go slowly. When your graft is complete, it should be absolutely in-visible.

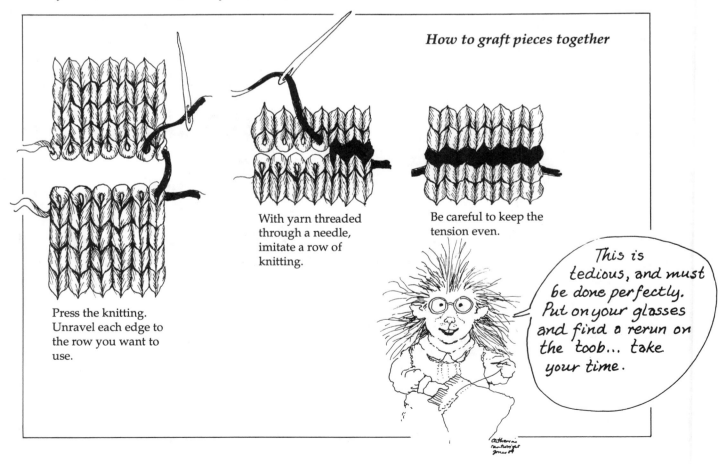

How to graft pieces together

Press the knitting. Unravel each edge to the row you want to use.

With yarn threaded through a needle, imitate a row of knitting.

Be careful to keep the tension even.

This is tedious, and must be done perfectly. Put on your glasses and find a rerun on the toob... take your time.

Useful seam variations

There are three basic types of seams—by "seam" I mean you go to your sewing machine and sew along what is or will be an edge of your fabric. Seams in this sense are used either to finish or to join edges. The simplest variation is the selvedge seam, which joins two finished edges. Then there's the binding seam, which secures the stitches on the edge of plain fabric or ribbing. Finally, there's the shaping seam, where you stitch your way quickly into a half-fashioned, nicely detailed garment. The diagrams explain how to master these alternatives.

Creeping shoulders. Some seams won't hold their shape, and need further persuasion. This information applies especially to the shoulder seams on some drop-shoulder sweaters, although you could find the technique useful elsewhere. Certain knits are prone to stretching or creeping when you zigzag a shoulder seam. Firm knits won't give you a problem, but anticipate trouble with soft and stretchy knits, fine fabrics, or very loose cloth. There's a simple solution, which can be applied either before or after the problem occurs.

If you foresee difficulty, you can add a stabiliz-ing piece of yarn to the seam as you stitch it. You'll need two pieces of the same yarn you knitted with, one for each shoulder. Pin one end of the first piece to one end of your seam-to-be, and wrap the yarn in a figure-eight around the pin so it won't slip. Measure the yarn, to locate the correct shoulder measurement. Align this point with the other end of the shoulder seam. Insert a pin at that end and wrap another figure-eight that won't shift around. Secure the yarn with a couple of additional pins in the middle of the soon-to-be seam. Press this endeavor with a little steam. Zigzag exactly over the yarn. Now it won't stretch. Finish the seam the way you would any other shoulder seam.

If you have just found out the hard way that your shoulder is drooping, after you have worn the garment, you can still tuck up the seam. Pin yarn over the stretched seam, adjusting it to the correct length. Secure the yarn ends and the middle as described above. Iron with plenty of steam, until you've eased all the stretching onto the yarn, then zigzag everything in place. You may also want to re-sew the straight stitching. Now it's all fixed.

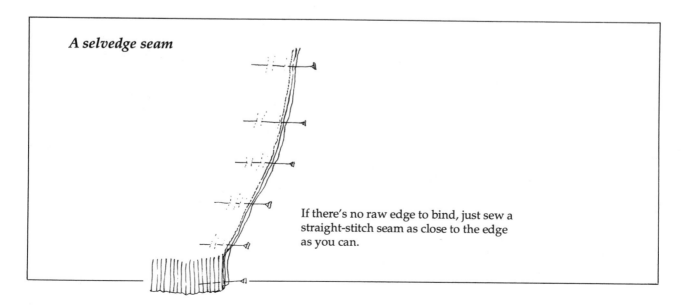

A selvedge seam

If there's no raw edge to bind, just sew a straight-stitch seam as close to the edge as you can.

A binding seam

Zigzag an edge of knitting that you would ordinarily bind off. Make sure you don't stretch the edge as you sew it, or it will ripple and look bad.

Or, zigzag an edge of ribbing that would otherwise be bound off. If the ribbing is intended to stretch, as a collar band must, stretch it out as you zigzag. It will ripple, but the ripples will disappear when you stretch and sew the ribbing in place on the garment.

A shaping seam

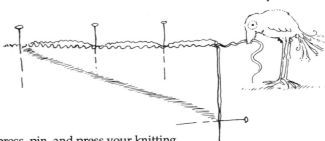

1. Align, press, pin, and press your knitting. Measure to get the seam in the right place. Chalk in the seamline.

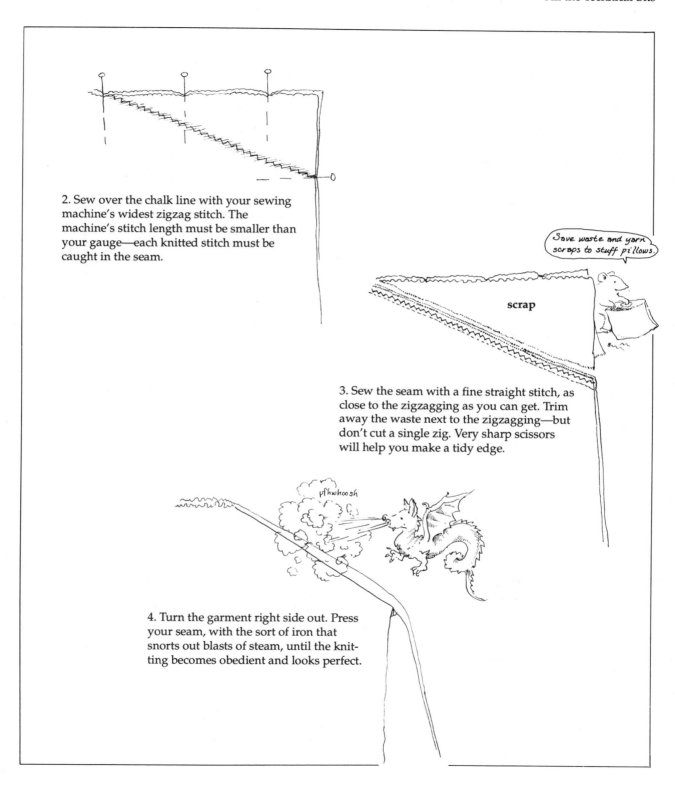

2. Sew over the chalk line with your sewing machine's widest zigzag stitch. The machine's stitch length must be smaller than your gauge—each knitted stitch must be caught in the seam.

Save waste and yarn scraps to stuff pillows.

scrap

3. Sew the seam with a fine straight stitch, as close to the zigzagging as you can get. Trim away the waste next to the zigzagging—but don't cut a single zig. Very sharp scissors will help you make a tidy edge.

pfhwhoosh

4. Turn the garment right side out. Press your seam, with the sort of iron that snorts out blasts of steam, until the knitting becomes obedient and looks perfect.

To prevent shoulder seams from stretching....

If your knit fabric is fine, soft, loose, or just inclined to stretch when you zigzag, construct a shoulder seam that will make it stay put.

Wrap the yarn in a figure-8 around the end pins.

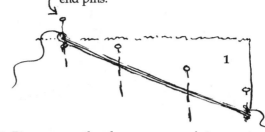

1. Pin yarn exactly where your seam is to go and secure it with a pin at each end of the seam. You'll probably want to measure to be sure the seam is exactly the right length.

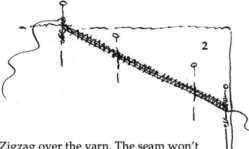

2. Zigzag over the yarn. The seam won't creep and stretch.

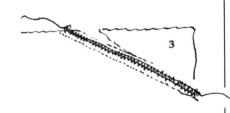

3. Finish the seam as usual.

To fix shoulder seams that have stretched after they were sewn....

If you find out the hard way, after the sweater is finished, that the knit fabric stretches, you can fix the problem.

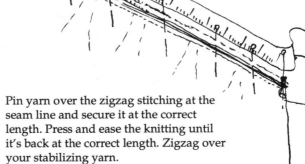

Pin yarn over the zigzag stitching at the seam line and secure it at the correct length. Press and ease the knitting until it's back at the correct length. Zigzag over your stabilizing yarn.

The neckline and collar department

Any sweater has to have an opening at the top; otherwise it will be very stuffy, you will bump into walls, and you will find it hard to eat pizza. A gash across the top would do, but looks crude. We are an elegant and clever species, and we prefer finished necklines, many with collars.

Finished necklines must do one thing perfectly. They must open up enough to get your head through. Ribbing is stretchy, so it opens up. Buttons unbutton, and open up. Shawl collars unfold, and open up. V-collars have a long circumference that is already open enough. Zippered fronts unzip. If you can't get the thing on over your head, you can't wear it; so the neckline has to be done right.

Getting a neckline to work while full-fashioning

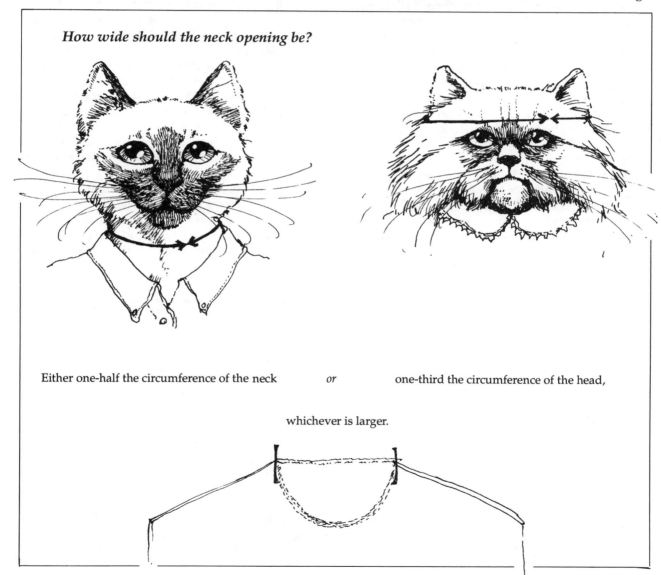

How wide should the neck opening be?

Either one-half the circumference of the neck   *or*   one-third the circumference of the head,

whichever is larger.

is tedious and uncertain. The shaping is a bother to calculate and then twiddle into shape with your tools. If you half-fashion a neckline, you can measure and chalk it into shape—and even change your mind a few times about the look you want—before you stitch and cut the fabric.

Crewneck finishes. When you have sewn the shoulders of your sweater, vest, or cape, mark the width of the neck hole. This is either half the circumference of the neck, or one-third the circumference of the head—whichever is larger. Enter that measurement on your fabric and chalk it in. The shape of the crewneck opening in the front is a semicircle or a parabola or any less mathematical curve that looks even and is about the same shape as your favorite crewneck. It should be 4" or 5" deep. The shape of a crewneck opening in back is a shallow curve that goes down about ½".

When you've got a crewneck chalk line that you like, zigzag all the way around. Cut away the extra fabric.

How much ribbing do you need? The ribbing piece has to stretch wide enough to go over your head. Calculate the gauge from the ribbing section of your sample swatch when it's stretched out wide. Figure out how many stitches you need in order to have the fabric stretch around your head. Knit your ribbing that many stitches wide, plus a little extra for a seam allowance or a fresh coiffure.

Knit 2" to 4" of rows, to taste. Don't bother to cast off the ribbing; just zigzag the edge and full the fabric.

If your garments are chronically tight around the neck, take the gauge of your ribbing when scrootched, not stretched. Measure your neck. Multiply the inches around your neck by the stitches per inch of the scrootched ribbing, and knit your collar band to this width. Sew the ribbing piece into a circle and pin it to the neck hole. To get it in evenly, divide both the neck opening and the circle of ribbing into quarters with pins, matching the quarters as you pin them together. Stretch both ribbing and sweater until they lie smoothly against each other as you sew them. Stitch them together, keeping the seam as close to the edge as you can while still catching everything securely.

Whatever type of ribbing you use, press the seam with lots of steam until it looks smooth. Open out the garment and encourage the ribbing to make a flat circle, with the ribbing radiating as neatly as cartoon sunrays—press and steam, steam and press.

If the ribbing does not snug back in when you stretch it out to pull it over your head, instead lying about your neck looking forlorn, you will need to sew in some elastic thread (see page 36). (You could also reknit, working at a tighter gauge.)

A *parabola* is a very good shape for a neckline. This is how to make a parabola with a necklace.

How much ribbing is enough?

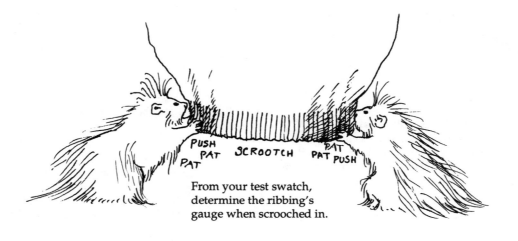

From your test swatch, determine the ribbing's gauge when scrooched in.

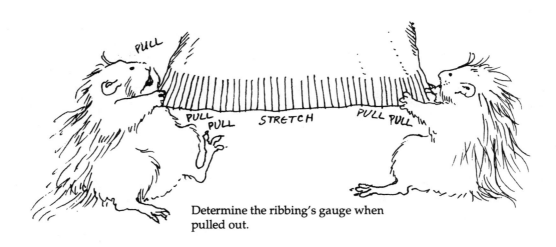

Determine the ribbing's gauge when pulled out.

To determine how much ribbing you need, measure where it's to go, and decide whether you'll need scrooched or stretched ribbing, or a compromise between the two.

For instance, the ribbing on a crew neck must scrootch in enough to snuggle against the neck, and stretch enough to pull on over the head.

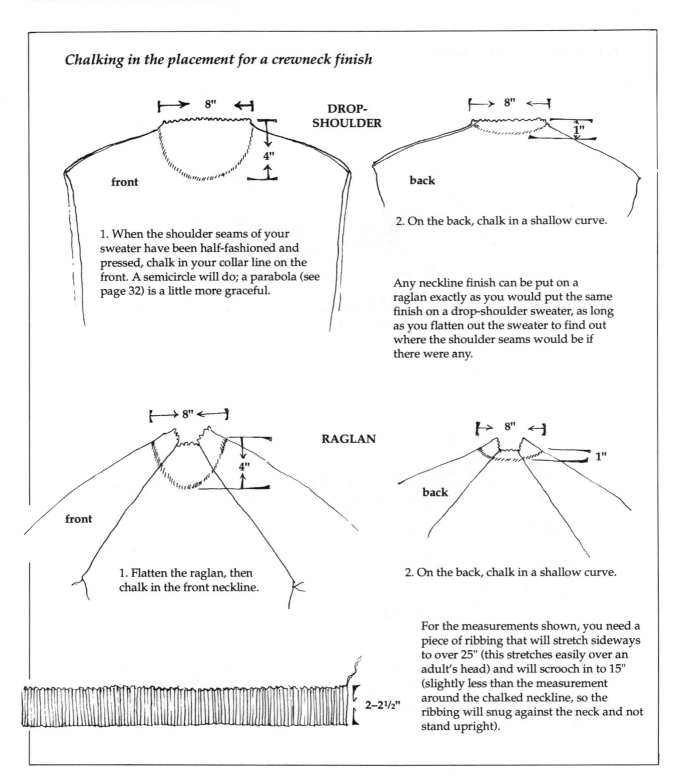

Chalking in the placement for a crewneck finish

DROP-SHOULDER

8"

4"

front

1. When the shoulder seams of your sweater have been half-fashioned and pressed, chalk in your collar line on the front. A semicircle will do; a parabola (see page 32) is a little more graceful.

8"

1"

back

2. On the back, chalk in a shallow curve.

Any neckline finish can be put on a raglan exactly as you would put the same finish on a drop-shoulder sweater, as long as you flatten out the sweater to find out where the shoulder seams would be if there were any.

RAGLAN

8"

4"

front

1. Flatten the raglan, then chalk in the front neckline.

8"

1"

back

2. On the back, chalk in a shallow curve.

For the measurements shown, you need a piece of ribbing that will stretch sideways to over 25" (this stretches easily over an adult's head) and will scrooch in to 15" (slightly less than the measurement around the chalked neckline, so the ribbing will snug against the neck and not stand upright).

2–2½"

Putting a crewneck on a sweater

1. Zigzag around your chalked neckline, and trim away the extra fabric.

2. Zigzag the unfinished edge of the ribbing. Stretch the ribbing as you zigzag.

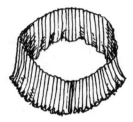

3. Sew the ribbing into a tube, with the narrowest possible seam.

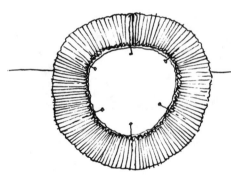

4. Pin the collar into the neck hole.

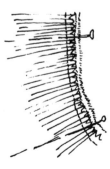

5. Stretch the ribbing and the knitting as you sew them together. Sew as close to the zigzagging as you can get.

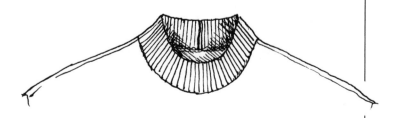

6. Press the collar with great blasts of steam until it looks wonderful.

If your ribbing goes floppo....

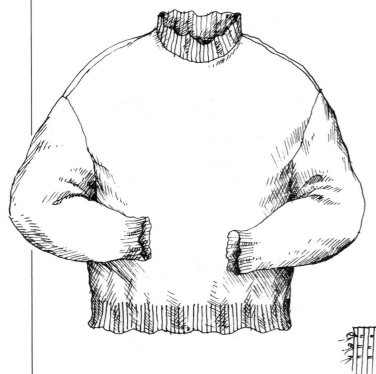

This is a common difficulty with cotton, silk, and kempy (or rough) wool.

Run elastic thread through the ribs on the inside, so the stitches don't show on the outside. Several rows of elastic sewn through and moderately stretched are better than one row tweaked up tight.

V-neck finishes. How far down should a V-neck go? As far as you want it. Point to where it should stop, and measure that length from your shoulder seam (see the illustration). Chalk that point on the front of your garment. The width of the opening at the shoulder seam should be half the circumference of your neck. Center that width on the fabric and chalk it in. Draw a V from the chalk marks to the point mark. On the back, chalk a shallow curve that drops only ½" down between the width marks. When you've got the chalk line the way you want it, zigzag it. Cut away the extra fabric.

How much ribbing do you need? Stretch out the ribbing on your sample swatch, but not so far that it feels strained. Figure its gauge when stretched. Measure all the way around the V. Multiply the V measurement by the stitches per inch of stretched ribbing. Cast on ribbing that many stitches wide and knit 2". Drop the fabric off the machine, zigzag the edge, and full the knitting.

Pin the ribbing around the neck opening. Divide both ribbing and neck opening in quarters so you can apply the finish evenly. Steam and press the ribbing and the garment together, encouraging the ribbing to stretch out. Sew the ribbing and garment together, stretching both fabrics until they lie smoothly against each other. Keep the seam as close to the edge as possible. Sew the V as nearly closed as you can. Neaten it up when you hand sew the crossover.

Remove the pins and coax the ribbing into not puckering the sweater by pressing with plenty of steam. Hand stitch the crossover at the point of the V.

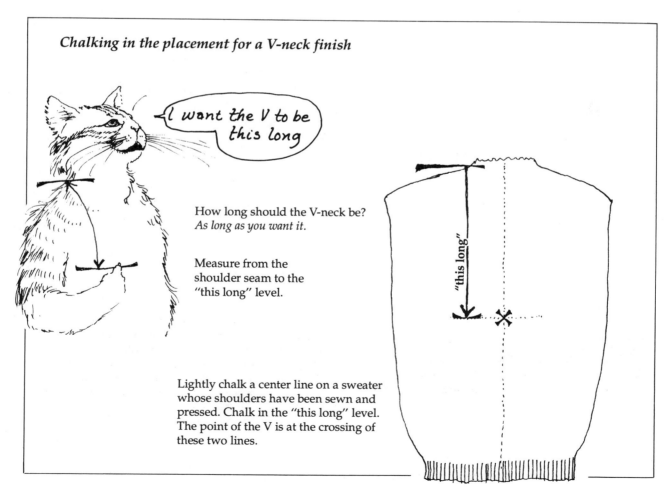

Chalking in the placement for a V-neck finish

I want the V to be this long

How long should the V-neck be? *As long as you want it.*

Measure from the shoulder seam to the "this long" level.

Lightly chalk a center line on a sweater whose shoulders have been sewn and pressed. Chalk in the "this long" level. The point of the V is at the crossing of these two lines.

"this long"

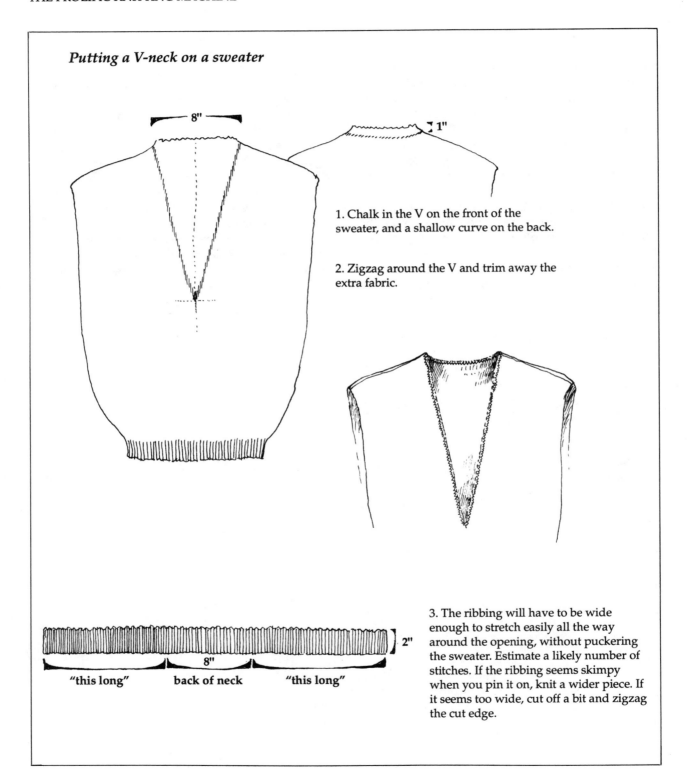

Putting a V-neck on a sweater

1. Chalk in the V on the front of the sweater, and a shallow curve on the back.

2. Zigzag around the V and trim away the extra fabric.

3. The ribbing will have to be wide enough to stretch easily all the way around the opening, without puckering the sweater. Estimate a likely number of stitches. If the ribbing seems skimpy when you pin it on, knit a wider piece. If it seems too wide, cut off a bit and zigzag the cut edge.

"this long"   back of neck   "this long"

4. Zigzag the unfinished edge of your ribbing. Stretch it as you zigzag.

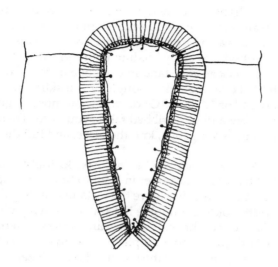

5. Pin the ribbing onto the V opening. If there's a little puckering that flattens out easily with a few blasts of your steam iron, you're fine. If the puckering won't flatten out even when you pull, knit a wider piece. If the ribbing seems flaccid instead of stretchy, you've got too much. Cut some off and bind the cut edge. When you've got the ribbing looking about right, sew it—close to the zigzagging—stretching it as you sew.

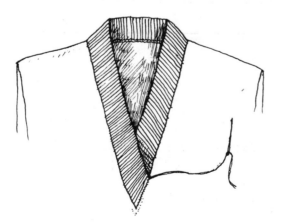

6. Unpin everything and press the V, stretching as you press, until the neckline looks smooth.

Hand sew the overlaps of the ribbing, inside and out. Press and stretch everything again, with great huffings of steam, until it looks memorable.

If your ribbing is obstinate about puckering, dampen it and hang a weight at the point of the V. A few fishing weights in a net bag on a Christmas ornament hook provides discipline for unruly ribbing. Let the sweater hang overnight.

A shawl collar. Shawl collars are reassuring for the shy, comforting to those who like a little cuddling, and essential for those who loathe the wind-chill factors in the snow belt. Different yarns behave very distinctly in the standing-up or flopping-down of a shawl collar. Check the character of your yarn with a large, fulled swatch of ribbing. Handle your swatch—fold it, stretch it—so you can see whether it will make a high-standing or a low-lying collar. Rub the swatch on your cheek a while, so you can find out whether it will feel cuddly or annoying when you wear it; if it's scratchy, you won't want a tight, high collar.

How far down should your shawl collar go? As far as you want. Point to how far down the front it should go. Measure from there to the point on your body where your shoulder seam will lie, and chalk that depth on your garment.

How wide across should the bottom of the shawl be? Stand in front of a mirror and imagine what would look best. Measure that width and chalk it on your garment.

How wide should the neck opening be at the shoulderline? The width should be one-half the circumference of your neck. Center that measurement on your garment and chalk it in.

Now make a chalkline connecting these marks on the front of your garment. On the back, make a shallow curve that dips down only ½". Zigzag your chalked neckline. Cut away the extra fabric.

Measure around your neckline to see how much ribbing you need. From pulling and relaxing your swatch of ribbing, you will be able to decide whether you want the collar to be very stretched or only slightly stretched: very stretched ribbing pulls up around your neck, while slightly stretched ribbing lies away from it. Decide how deep you want the ribbing to be by holding your swatch up to your neck as you stand in front of a mirror. Does 6" folded over look like enough, or is it skimpy? How does 8" or 10" look? Or do you want more? Figure how big a piece of ribbed fabric you need. Then determine your gauge, knit the piece, and full the fabric.

A shawl collar is wide in the back, doubled over, but has to get narrower in front to fit into the opening. You can either leave the rectangle at its full width, folding it double in front and sewing it in place, or cut the ends so they are narrower in front. In both cases, the front pieces cross over each other at the opening. For the second choice, zigzag the shape and cut off the extra fabric.

A few shawl collars

—the squared sort

How far down should the shawl go?
As far as you want it.

How "shawly" should the collar be?
A little fold—rib 5"
Snuggly—rib 7"
Deep—rib 9"
Enough to hide in—rib 11"

Pin the collar into the neckline. Press and stretch the collar and body together, then sew them, keeping them stretched so they lie smoothly against each other. For the rectangular, folded collar, you will have four layers of collar fabric at the front opening. For the shaped collar, you will have two layers. Take out the pins and press and steam the seam until it is very neat. Sew the crossover in place by hand, using the same yarn you used to knit the collar. Gently steam the collar fold so it rolls over nicely.

A very long shawl collar. If the neckline opening is much bigger around than your knitting machine bed can manage to knit widthwise, switch directions and knit the collar lengthwise. This ribbing will lie flatter, and you won't stretch it out as you sew it into place. Otherwise, proceed as usual.

A shawl collar that comes to a point. Chalk the garment as if you were making a V-neck collar. Prepare the collar and sew it in just as you would for other shawl collars.

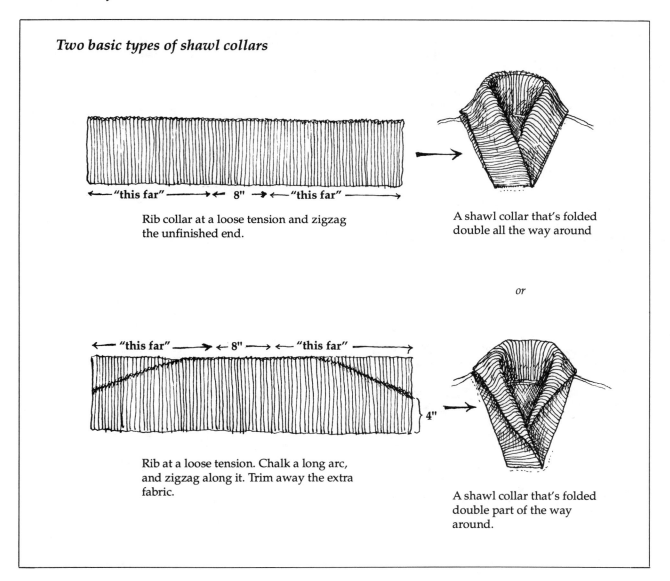

Two basic types of shawl collars

←— "this far" —→ ← 8" → ←— "this far" —→

Rib collar at a loose tension and zigzag the unfinished end.

A shawl collar that's folded double all the way around

or

←— "this far" —→ ← 8" —→ ←— "this far" —→

4"

Rib at a loose tension. Chalk a long arc, and zigzag along it. Trim away the extra fabric.

A shawl collar that's folded double part of the way around.

Putting a shawl collar on a sweater

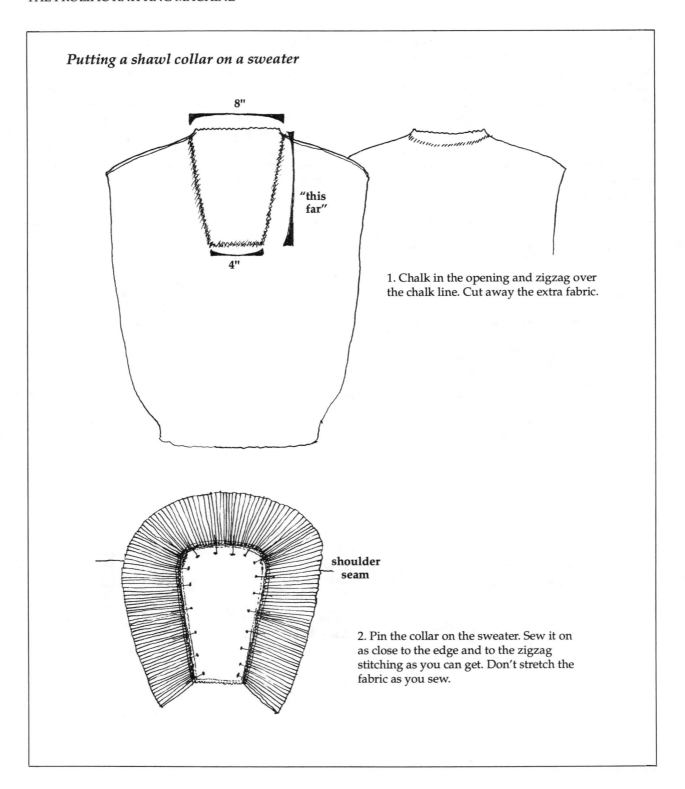

1. Chalk in the opening and zigzag over the chalk line. Cut away the extra fabric.

shoulder seam

2. Pin the collar on the sweater. Sew it on as close to the edge and to the zigzag stitching as you can get. Don't stretch the fabric as you sew.

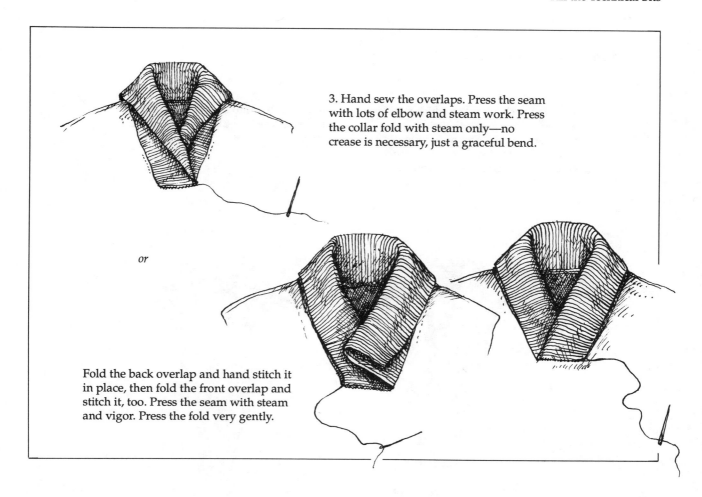

3. Hand sew the overlaps. Press the seam with lots of elbow and steam work. Press the collar fold with steam only—no crease is necessary, just a graceful bend.

or

Fold the back overlap and hand stitch it in place, then fold the front overlap and stitch it, too. Press the seam with steam and vigor. Press the fold very gently.

A shawl collar knitted lengthwise

If you want a shawl collar which is longer than your knitting machine can handle widthwise, knit the ribbing lengthwise. This collar will lie flatter than the other sort, and is less likely to give you pucker problems.

Sew the collar into the neck opening in the same way as the other shawl collars are attached.

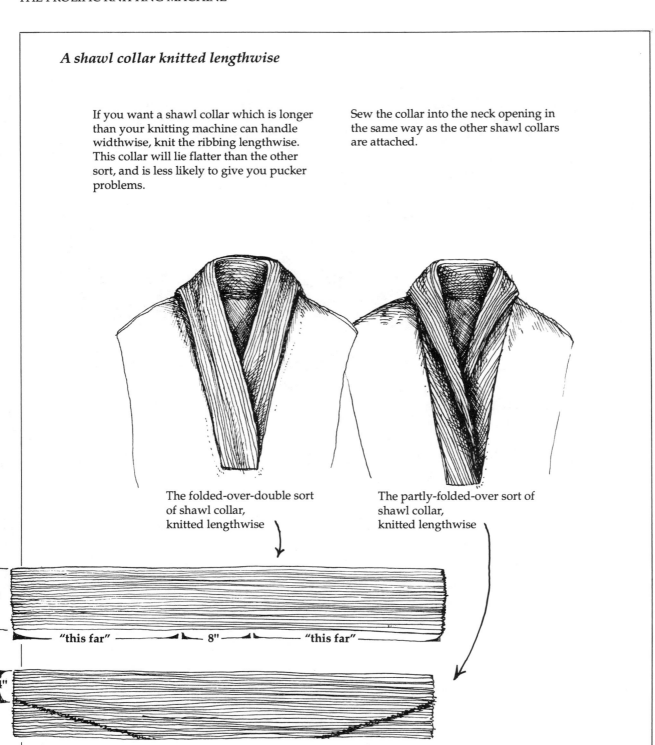

The folded-over-double sort of shawl collar, knitted lengthwise

The partly-folded-over sort of shawl collar, knitted lengthwise

8"

"this far" — 8" — "this far"

4"

A V-neck shawl collar

A shawl collar can be laid into a V neckline. Prepare and sew the V as on other V-neck sweaters, and hand sew the overlap as usual.

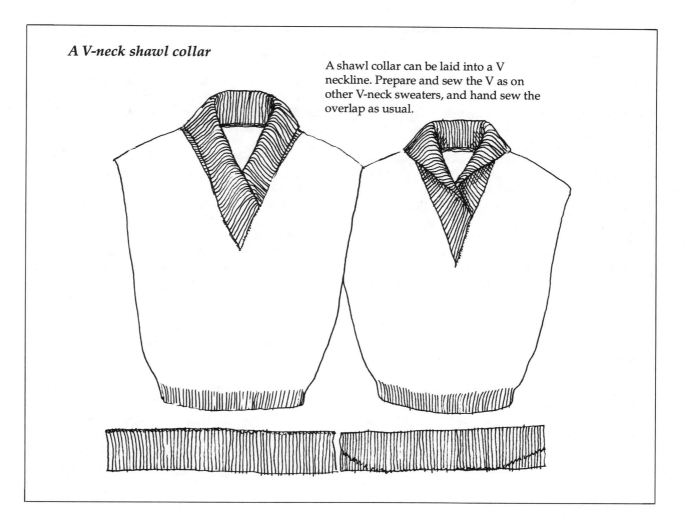

Buttoning up

There are many ways to knit buttonholes. Here is one that is quick, adaptable, and makes a firm sort of buttonhole. It runs up-and-down in the fabric (buttonholes can also run side-to-side). This technique results in a doubled-over button band, and it works best for the fabric made on a standard (rather than bulky) knitting machine. Variations for use with bulky fabrics start on page 53.

The buttonholes are produced by making a knitted edging with pairs of holes. The holes are made by dividing the knitting into unequal sections, then knitting each section separately while the other two sections are in holding position. The completed edging is folded in half and topstitched onto the garment; you secure the inside edge first, and then the outside edge. The paired holes are matched up and stitched together to form the buttonholes. It's easier than it sounds.

Try a few buttonholes. First, make some practice buttonholes, with a real project in mind. How big do you need a buttonhole to be? Measure across a button you want to use. Then, from your gauge numbers, figure out how many rows long the buttonhole should be. You will need to knit the hole a little longer than that, because it will contract a bit when you finish it.

The illustrations show how to knit the first quarter, the middle half, and then the last quarter of the buttonhole, placing the other sections on hold as you work. Try knitting a few sample buttonholes, to get the feel of knitting the little sections separately without jumbling up or dropping the stitches. Then see which buttonhole fits best.

How wide should the buttonhole strip be? I like to make it between 1½" and 2" wide, before it is folded in half. It can't be much narrower, but it could be wider. Look at your gauge, and choose a number of stitches that is evenly divisible by four and produces a fabric in that width range.

Prepare the sweater. Chalk a line down the center front of a garment that is ready to have its neckline finish added—before the finish goes on. This means that the shoulders have been seamed together. Chalk in the neckhole, the same way you would for a crewneck or V-neck. Zigzag up one side of the center line, around the neck opening, and down the other side of the center line. Cut the front open between the two center-front zigzag lines.

Place a few buttons on the sweater, to see how many look good. When there are as many as you like, space them exactly as far apart as you want them to be, and measure the distance between them. Figure out how many rows of knitting will occur between each button and its neighbors.

Knit the buttonhole band. To work the band, cast on and knit a few inches. The exact number of rows is not critical because you will finish the end after the band is attached to the garment. Knit one buttonhole. Knit the number of rows you need to reach the next buttonhole, and knit that buttonhole. Work the rows to the next buttonhole, and so on, until you have as many buttonholes as you need.

Count the number of rows aloud as you go, because with all the holding-position rows, your counter will go wildly off. It's hard to remember to reset it at the end of each hole.

Measure the rest of the way around the neck opening, and down the other half of the front. Knit along on your strip, without any fancy maneuvers, until you have worked that many inches, plus a few.

Full and press the band.

Sew on the buttonhole band. Position the top buttonhole just below the corner of the neckhole, on the inside of the garment. The outside of the buttonhole band will face you. Men's buttonhole bands are applied to the left front piece, and women's to the right front piece ("left" and "right" are determined by the position as the sweater will be worn). Press and smooth the buttonhole part of the strip down to the bottom. Be sure the strips up and down the front are not stretched to fit, or the front of the sweater will pucker.

When you have the buttonholes evenly in place, pin them all down. Pin the band at the edge of the center opening, just covering the zigzag stitching, so that the buttonholes are clear of the cut edge. If you sew the band too far in, the buttonholes will be full of cut yarn ends, or worse, blocked entirely.

When you pin the band around the neck opening, *do* stretch it slightly. The neck needs to be eased in, but not puckered.

Then pin the band down the other front edge, being careful *not* to stretch that part.

Press the pinned-on band, and topstitch its inside edge, keeping the seam right on the line of stitches at the edge. Remove the pins, and fold the band in half onto the front side. Center each buttonhole over its mate and pin them together.

Pin the rest of the band in place, just covering the zigzagging and the topstitched seam. Press the band. Topstitch the band again, on the outside,

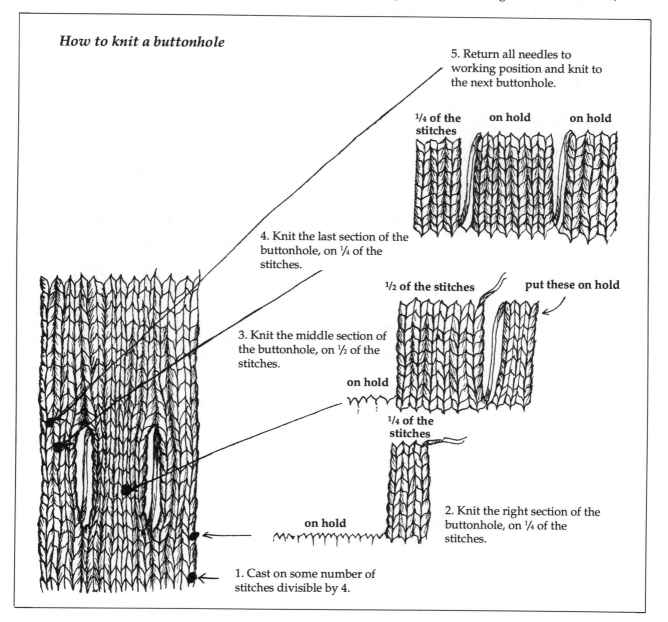

How to knit a buttonhole

5. Return all needles to working position and knit to the next buttonhole.

¹⁄₄ of the stitches   on hold   on hold

4. Knit the last section of the buttonhole, on ¹⁄₄ of the stitches.

¹⁄₂ of the stitches   put these on hold

3. Knit the middle section of the buttonhole, on ¹⁄₂ of the stitches.

on hold

¹⁄₄ of the stitches

2. Knit the right section of the buttonhole, on ¹⁄₄ of the stitches.

on hold

1. Cast on some number of stitches divisible by 4.

keeping your stitches along the line of stitches at the edge. Remove the pins and press the band again.

Unravel the bottom ends of the band until they are even with the bottom edge of the garment. Finish the ends of the band by sewing them closed, matching stitch to stitch as shown.

Whipstitch around the buttonholes, sewing the front hole to the back hole and tucking the X yarns to the inside.

Sew on the buttons.

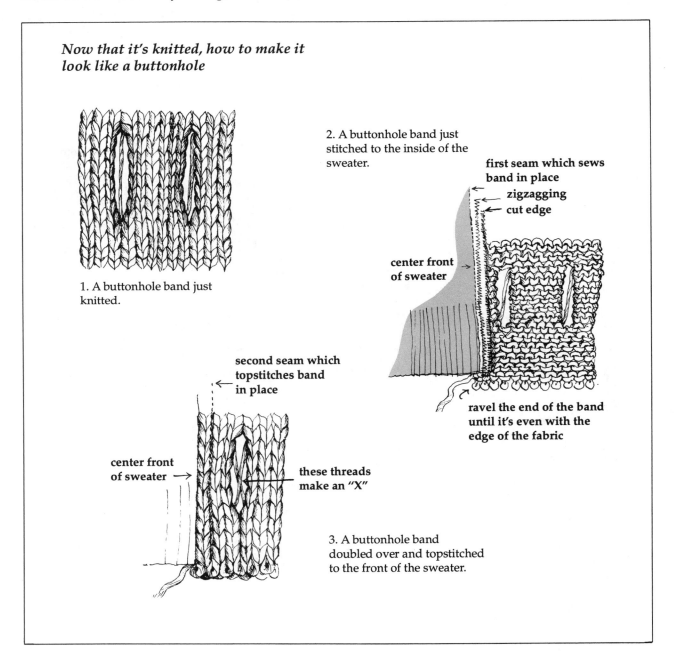

Now that it's knitted, how to make it look like a buttonhole

1. A buttonhole band just knitted.

2. A buttonhole band just stitched to the inside of the sweater.

first seam which sews band in place
zigzagging
cut edge
center front of sweater

ravel the end of the band until it's even with the edge of the fabric

second seam which topstitches band in place

center front of sweater

these threads make an "X"

3. A buttonhole band doubled over and topstitched to the front of the sweater.

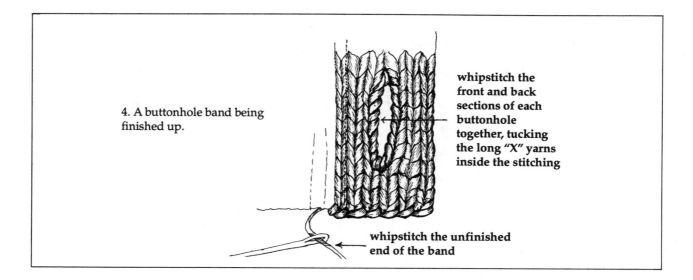

4. A buttonhole band being finished up.

whipstitch the front and back sections of each buttonhole together, tucking the long "X" yarns inside the stitching

whipstitch the unfinished end of the band

How big to knit a buttonhole

Find a button you love.

Knit a buttonhole a little longer than the button.

Whipstitch the buttonhole; this will make it smaller and tighter. See if the button fits.

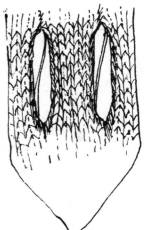

Try a few buttonholes, both a little smaller and a little larger than the size you think is a likely fit. One is bound to be snug and right. With a little practice, you'll knit these little varmints smoothly.

Preparing a sweater for a button band

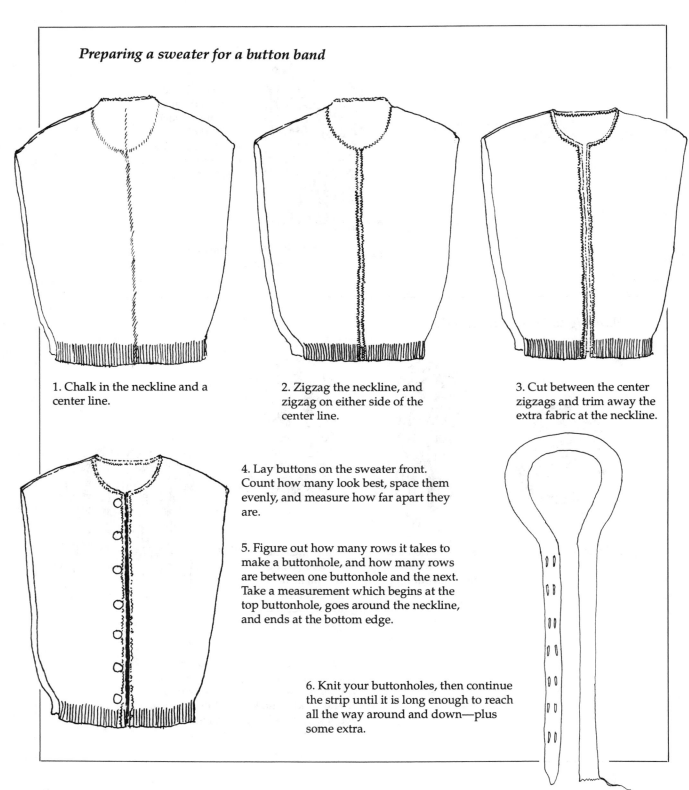

1. Chalk in the neckline and a center line.

2. Zigzag the neckline, and zigzag on either side of the center line.

3. Cut between the center zigzags and trim away the extra fabric at the neckline.

4. Lay buttons on the sweater front. Count how many look best, space them evenly, and measure how far apart they are.

5. Figure out how many rows it takes to make a buttonhole, and how many rows are between one buttonhole and the next. Take a measurement which begins at the top buttonhole, goes around the neckline, and ends at the bottom edge.

6. Knit your buttonholes, then continue the strip until it is long enough to reach all the way around and down—plus some extra.

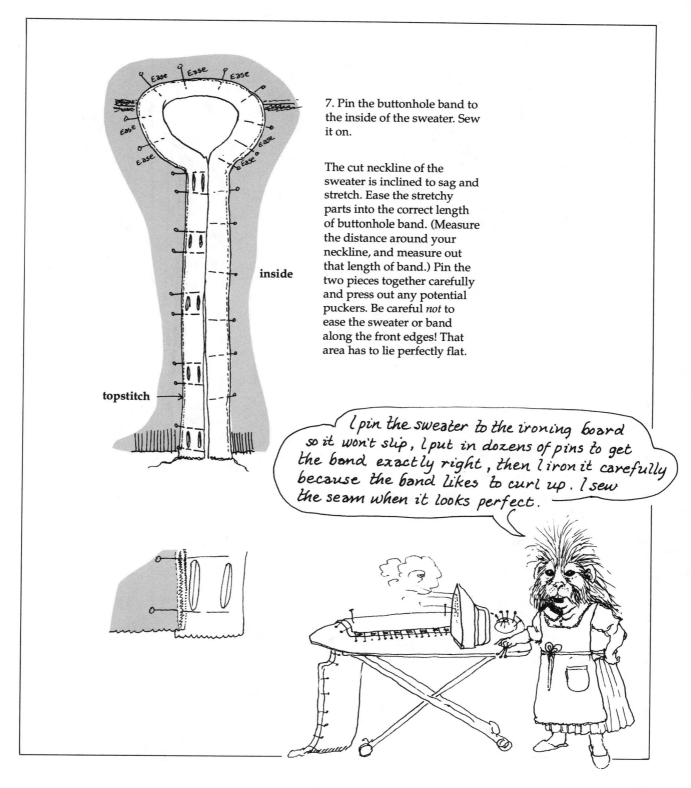

7. Pin the buttonhole band to the inside of the sweater. Sew it on.

The cut neckline of the sweater is inclined to sag and stretch. Ease the stretchy parts into the correct length of buttonhole band. (Measure the distance around your neckline, and measure out that length of band.) Pin the two pieces together carefully and press out any potential puckers. Be careful *not* to ease the sweater or band along the front edges! That area has to lie perfectly flat.

inside

topstitch

I pin the sweater to the ironing board so it won't slip, I put in dozens of pins to get the band exactly right, then I iron it carefully because the band likes to curl up. I sew the seam when it looks perfect.

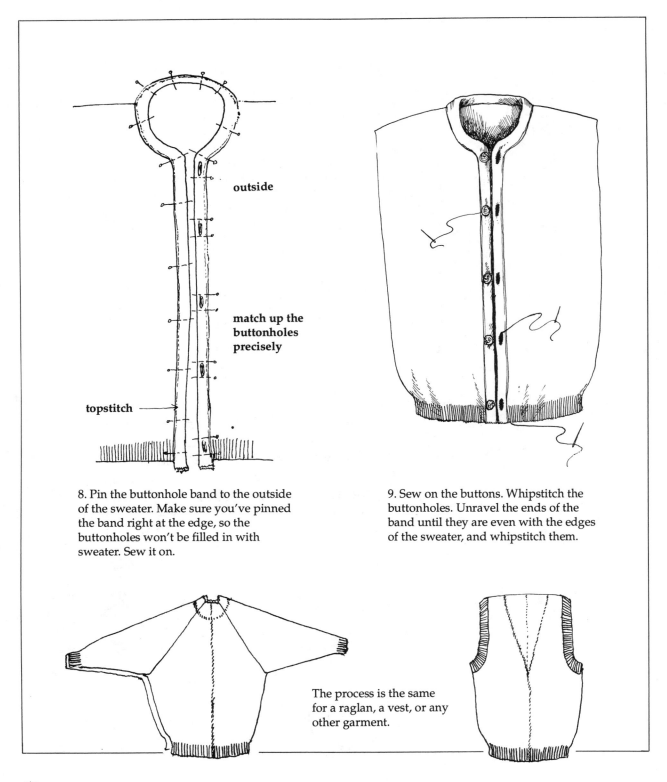

outside

match up the buttonholes precisely

topstitch

8. Pin the buttonhole band to the outside of the sweater. Make sure you've pinned the band right at the edge, so the buttonholes won't be filled in with sweater. Sew it on.

9. Sew on the buttons. Whipstitch the buttonholes. Unravel the ends of the band until they are even with the edges of the sweater, and whipstitch them.

The process is the same for a raglan, a vest, or any other garment.

The bulky options. Doubled bands don't work well with thick fabrics, so if you're using a bulky knitting machine you'll need a different approach to finishing the front edges of cardigans and to making buttonholes. These techniques require larger stitches and thicker fabric to work well; they are not recommended for the fabric produced by standard-gauge machines.

If your bulky knit is too thick for a folded-over band, consider a ribbed shawl collar. Begin by knitting a swatch of ribbing big enough to calculate your gauge.

Prepare the sweater as you would for a V-neck cardigan. Measure from the center point on the back neckline, down the V cut, to the bottom front of the sweater. You'll need two identical pieces of collar-and-band fabric, each made to this length and as wide as you want your collar to be. I use about an 8" width.

Do plan to make the collar in two pieces. Many machines do a ratty job of increasing on ribbing, but a tidy job of decreasing. It's also easier to get the decreases evenly matched on both sides if you've got a handy dividing line (the center back).

Check your gauge calculations. How many stitches should you cast on to get a wide shawl collar? How many rows will you need to knit to make each collar-and-band piece?

I keep the shawl collar at its maximum width from the center of the back neckline to halfway

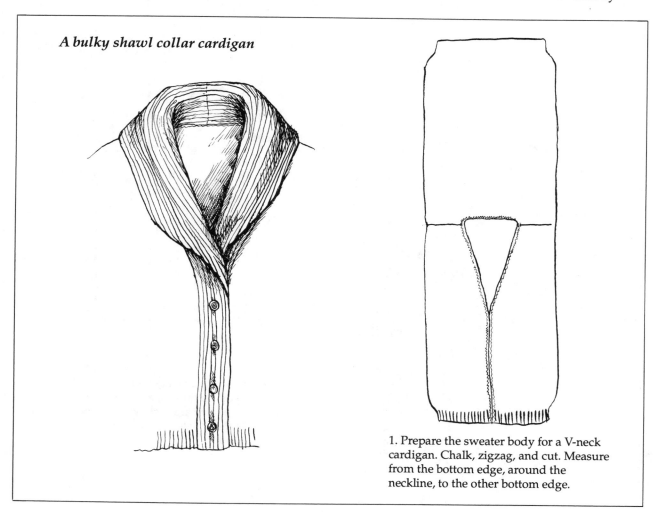

A bulky shawl collar cardigan

1. Prepare the sweater body for a V-neck cardigan. Chalk, zigzag, and cut. Measure from the bottom edge, around the neckline, to the other bottom edge.

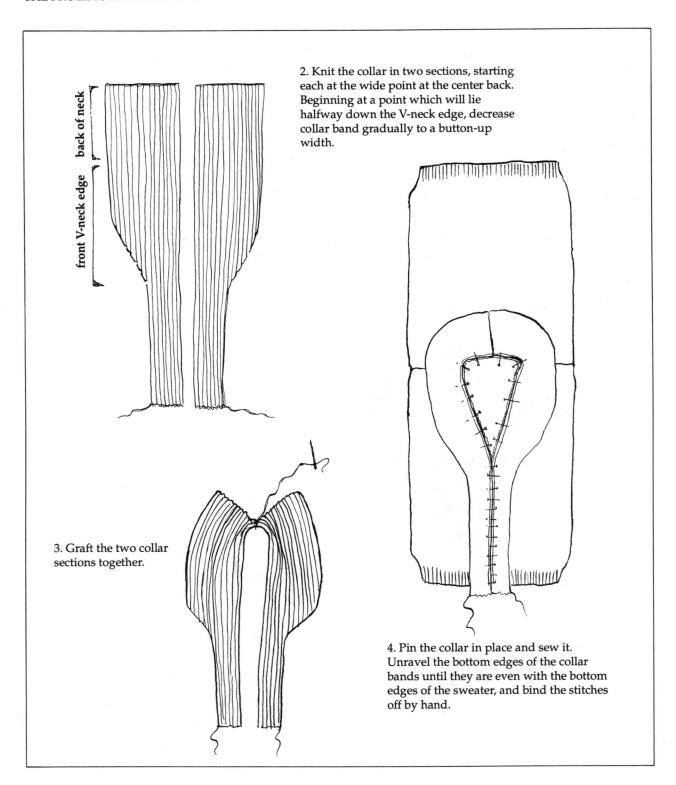

2. Knit the collar in two sections, starting each at the wide point at the center back. Beginning at a point which will lie halfway down the V-neck edge, decrease collar band gradually to a button-up width.

3. Graft the two collar sections together.

4. Pin the collar in place and sew it. Unravel the bottom edges of the collar bands until they are even with the bottom edges of the sweater, and bind the stitches off by hand.

down the V. Then I decrease one stitch on the outside edge every fourth row, until I've reduced the width of the fabric to 3". I continue knitting straight at that width until I've gone past the calculated length of the collar band; this leaves me with some buttoning-up room, and enough extra to ravel back so the bottom edges end up exactly even.

To the numbers you determined above, add the following: Where do you want to start decreasing? How far do you want to go beyond the hem of the sweater?

When you knit the two collar-and-band pieces, be sure you decrease on the left edge of one and the right edge of the other. When they're done,

graft them nicely together at the center back. Sew the collar-and-bands onto the prepared sweater, front and back. Press it into shape. Unravel the ends to the correct lengths and bind off the stitches by hand.

Decide where you want your buttonholes. Wiggle a fingertip through the fabric where you want a buttonhole, and keep wiggling until the hole's big enough for the tip of your thumb. Continue wiggling until you can get your button to pass in and out through the hole. Put your thumb back in, and with a needle and your knitting yarn work buttonhole stitches around the edge of the hole to hold it in place. This buttonhole doesn't get floppy like some buttonholes; it is adaptable and easy.

A buttonhole for bulky knits

1. Wiggle your fingertip in between stitches to start a buttonhole.

2. Keep wiggling until your thumb tip will go through.

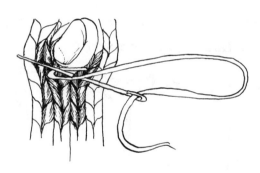

3. Check to see if your button fits, then buttonhole stitch around the hole.

4. One quick and easy bulky buttonhole!

Zipping up

Chalk, zigzag, and open the front of your sweater as you would for a buttoned-up garment. Unzip a separating zipper—the sort that's used on jackets. With the right side of the zipper against the right side of the sweater, and with the teeth pointing away from the center opening, set the bottoms of the zipper halves at the bottom edges of the sweater's front opening.

Pin the zipper halves carefully along the zigzag lines. If you have stripes or patterns that cross the front opening, be sure they will line up when you zip the garment together. Be careful not to stretch or pucker the sweater onto the zipper, and when you've got the halves positioned right, sew them onto the sweater. A zipper foot makes this easier to do with your sewing machine, or you can stitch the zipper in place by hand.

Take out the pins, turn the zipper halves so the teeth point toward the center opening, and zip up the sweater. Press the zipper seam with plenty of steam. Topstitch the sweater along both sides of the zipper, to keep the zipper tapes from rolling out and snagging.

That was easy enough, but you also need to add some sort of neckline finish to cover the untidiness at the top of the zipper. You can use an edging band and a hood for a cover, or you can knit a piece of crewneck-type ribbing twice as long (or deep) as usual, sew it into place, and fold it over to the inside. As you hand sew the ribbing around the inside, tuck the top bits of the zipper into the ribbing and make them disappear.

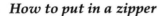

How to put in a zipper

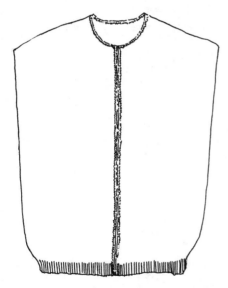

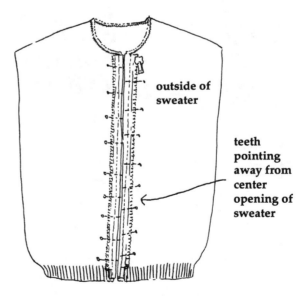

outside of sweater

teeth pointing away from center opening of sweater

1. Chalk, zigzag, and cut the sweater as you would for a buttoned cardigan.

2. Pin the two halves of a separating zipper in place, being careful not to stretch or pucker the knitting. If there are stripes or patterns in your sweater, be sure they will line up when the zipper is closed. Use a straight stitch to fasten down both halves of the zipper.

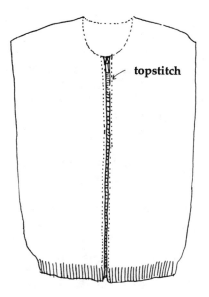

topstitch

3. Unpin the zipper and zip it up. Press the sweater back from the zipper, using plenty of steam. Topstitch the zipper so it will lie flat.

4½"

4. Knit a crewneck band 4½" long and zigzag the raw edge.

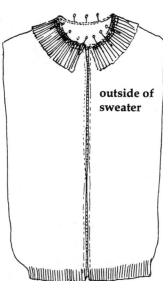

outside of sweater

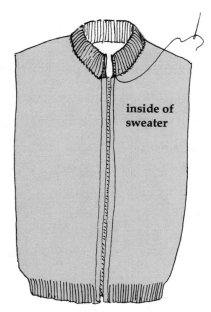

inside of sweater

5. Pin the crewneck band onto the outside of the sweater and sew it in place. Unpin it, and fold it over to the inside. Hand sew the collar all around the inside, and hand sew with yarn over the top edge of the zipper so it looks tidy.

6. Tuck the top bits of the zipper into the doubled crewneck band. Hand sew the band in place with yarn, and sew the top of the zipper inside the band.

Hoods

Hoods are tricky to attach to a sweater, but can be very worthwhile. If you're apt to lose fifteen caps on a playground, or are unable to fetch a dropped headwarmer from a wheelchair, a hood can be indispensable. Hoods are also necessary for the romantic and medieval.

Measure from the top of one shoulder near the neck, over the head, to the other shoulder. That's as wide as you need to knit the hood. Measure from eyebrows to crown, and add an inch or two for fluffy hair. That's the depth you need.

Knit a rectangle to these measurements, with 1½" of ribbing at the bottom, to surround the face. Don't bother to cast off at the top; the stitches will become the back seam. Full and press the piece of fabric.

Zigzag the unfinished edge. Then fold the fabric in half and sew the zigzagged edges together, to form the hood.

Prepare your sweater as if for a buttoned or zipped front opening. Sew along until you have applied the buttons or stitched the zipper in place, but the neck has only been chalked, zigzagged, and trimmed.

Knit two edging bands, each 1½" wide. Make the first measure the same as the circumference of your neck, plus 4". Make the other 48" long. Full and press these bands.

Pin the shorter band to the inside of the neck opening, slightly easing the sweater onto the band. Topstitch this band to the sweater.

Pin the hood to this band. The hood will need to be eased and gathered to fit the band, so use plenty of pins and position it evenly. Topstitch the band to the hood.

Pin the longer band to the outside of the sweater, over the inside band. Center it at the back—the extra length will tie in the front. Topstitch the second band carefully to the hood and sweater, keeping the line of stitches at the edge of the band.

Use the stitching methods of grafting to join the ends of the inside band to the outside one, neatly covering the edging of the buttonhole band or the top of the zipper, as well as the edges of the sweater and the hood. Where you don't have a raw edge to graft to, work the same stitches to make a neat join. Press the bands until they look like they grew where they have now been planted.

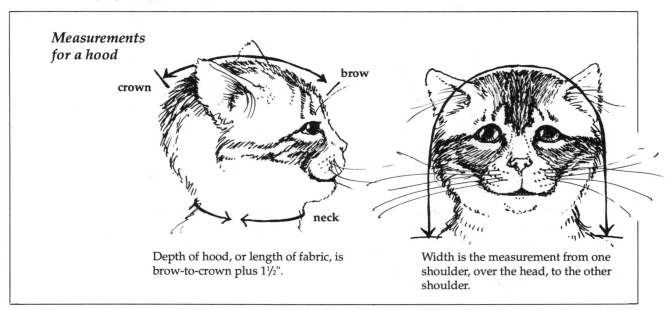

Measurements for a hood

crown   brow   neck

Depth of hood, or length of fabric, is brow-to-crown plus 1½".

Width is the measurement from one shoulder, over the head, to the other shoulder.

How to knit the hood and neck bands

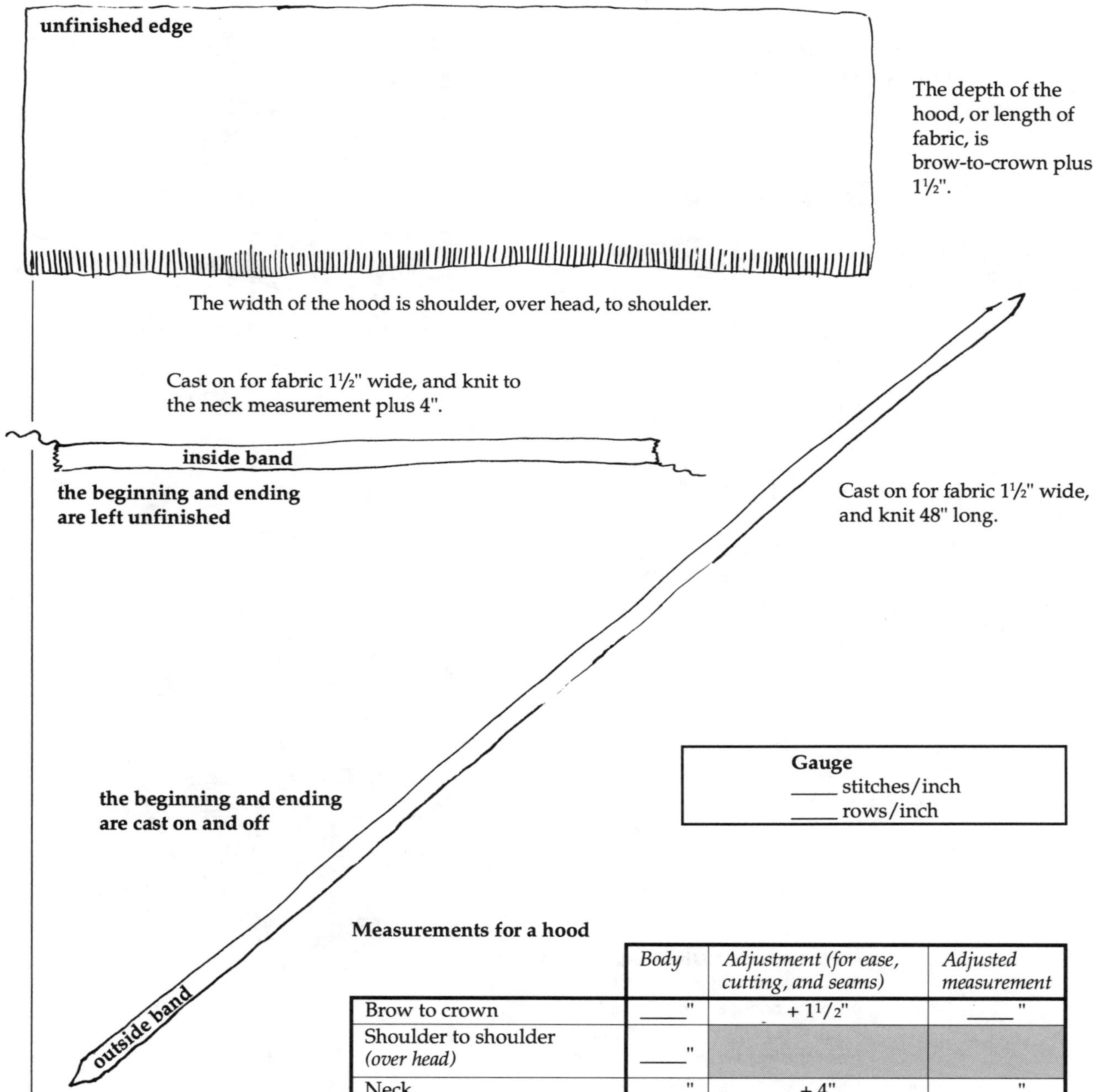

unfinished edge

The depth of the hood, or length of fabric, is brow-to-crown plus 1½".

The width of the hood is shoulder, over head, to shoulder.

Cast on for fabric 1½" wide, and knit to the neck measurement plus 4".

inside band

the beginning and ending are left unfinished

Cast on for fabric 1½" wide, and knit 48" long.

the beginning and ending are cast on and off

outside band

Gauge
_____ stitches/inch
_____ rows/inch

Measurements for a hood

	Body	Adjustment (for ease, cutting, and seams)	Adjusted measurement
Brow to crown	_____ "	+ 1½"	_____ "
Shoulder to shoulder *(over head)*	_____ "		
Neck	_____ "	+ 4"	_____ "

Putting a hood on a sweater

1. Prepare your sweater and finish the front edges with a buttonhole band or zipper. Leave the neck hole chalked, zigzagged, and trimmed.

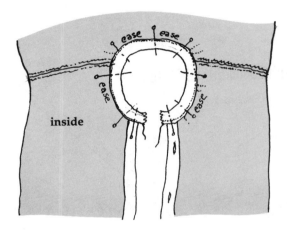

2. Pin the inside neck band to the inside of the neck hole. Ease the sweater into the band and press everything. Sew the edge of the band to the sweater.

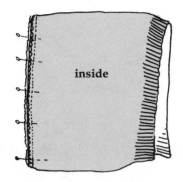

3. Fold the hood in half and zigzag up the unfinished edge. Sew up the back seam.

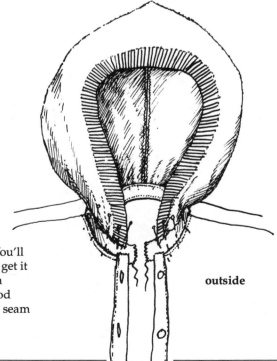

4. Pin the hood to the inside band. You'll need to tuck and gather the hood to get it onto the band; try to pin the tucks in evenly. Topstitch the band to the hood from the inside, so you can keep the seam right on the edge of the band.

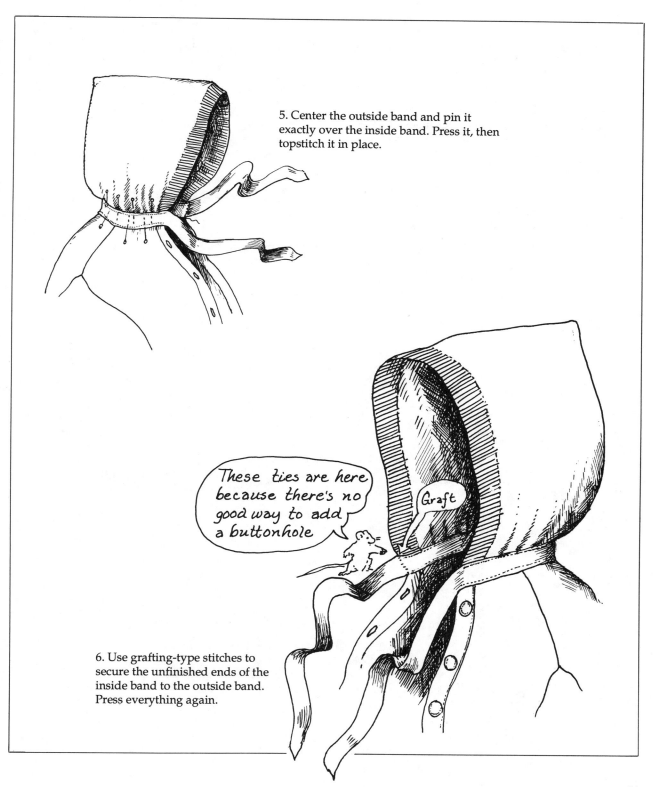

5. Center the outside band and pin it exactly over the inside band. Press it, then topstitch it in place.

These ties are here because there's no good way to add a buttonhole

Graft

6. Use grafting-type stitches to secure the unfinished ends of the inside band to the outside band. Press everything again.

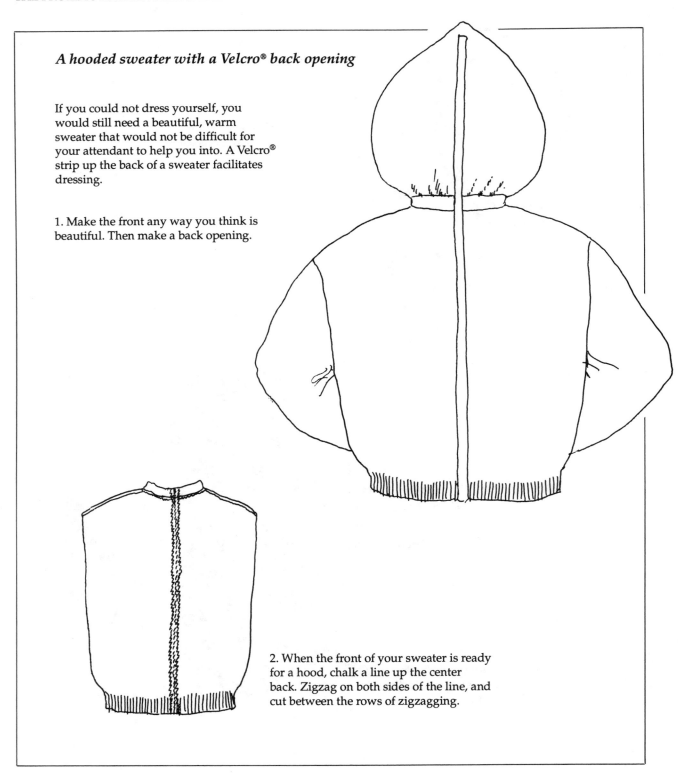

A hooded sweater with a Velcro® back opening

If you could not dress yourself, you would still need a beautiful, warm sweater that would not be difficult for your attendant to help you into. A Velcro® strip up the back of a sweater facilitates dressing.

1. Make the front any way you think is beautiful. Then make a back opening.

2. When the front of your sweater is ready for a hood, chalk a line up the center back. Zigzag on both sides of the line, and cut between the rows of zigzagging.

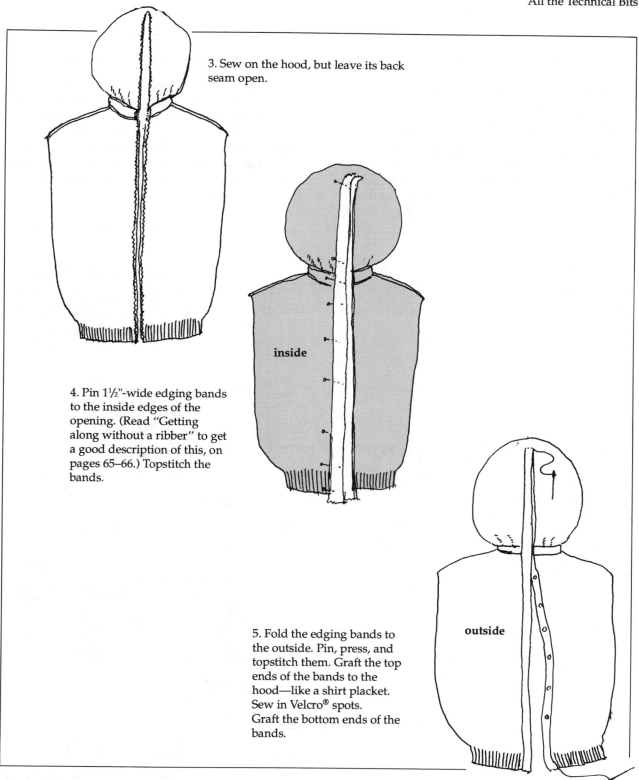

3. Sew on the hood, but leave its back seam open.

4. Pin 1½"-wide edging bands to the inside edges of the opening. (Read "Getting along without a ribber" to get a good description of this, on pages 65–66.) Topstitch the bands.

inside

5. Fold the edging bands to the outside. Pin, press, and topstitch them. Graft the top ends of the bands to the hood—like a shirt placket. Sew in Velcro® spots. Graft the bottom ends of the bands.

outside

Pockets

What do you want to put in your pocket? If you want to put your hand in your pocket, place it on a piece of paper and draw a rectangle around it, as big as you want your pocket to be. If you want a pocket for pens, car keys, gerbils, or ski wax, draw a rectangle around those. Does your hand need to get in to reach or pat these things? If so, include it.

Knit a rectangle to the size which will fit the objects to be pocketed. If you work ribbing at the top of the rectangle, the pocket won't be inclined to sag open. If you cast off the bottom, you can topstitch the pocket in place with your sewing machine—this is the most durable way to apply it. If you leave the bottom edge unfinished, you can graft the pocket to the sweater; this looks very pure and handmade, but the seam is no stronger than the yarn you use to work it.

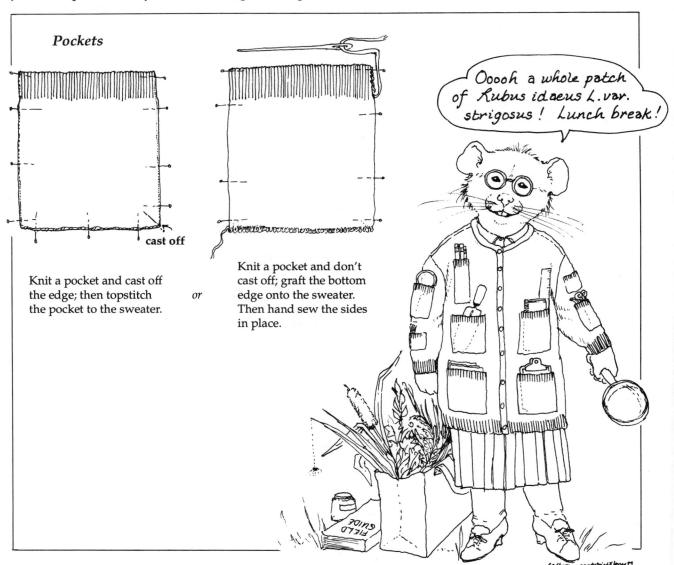

Pockets

cast off

Knit a pocket and cast off the edge; then topstitch the pocket to the sweater.

or

Knit a pocket and don't cast off; graft the bottom edge onto the sweater. Then hand sew the sides in place.

Ooooh a whole patch of *Rubus idaeus L. var. strigosus*! Lunch break!

Getting by without a ribber

If you don't have a ribber, you may be able to fake ribbing. The instruction book that came with your knitting machine showed you different ways to cast on, some of which made acceptable garment edges and some of which didn't. If you don't have a ribber, you may have tried a few mock ribs and hooked-up ribs, and you know whether or not you think they were worth the bother.

If not, there's another trick you can try. Look carefully at sweaters in shops. Some don't have ribbing. The manufacturers may not use ribbing because every ribber costs money, and a little clever design can save capital. What can you learn from these folks? One of their better tricks is binding an edge which would otherwise have ribbing with a knitted band—a lot of T-shirts have this. You can work edge bindings around a sweater's neck, hem, and/or sleeves.

Around the neck. Edge bindings are fine for cardigans, of course. The buttonhole band is a sort of edge binding. Because binding won't stretch, when you use it on a pullover you will need to make a scoop neckline or a V-neckline.

Knit an edging 1½" to 2" wide, to be folded in half. Work it a little longer than the neck opening's circumference. Full and press the band, and pin it to the inside of the sweater, around the zigzagged neck opening. Ease the knitting a bit into the binding, so the neckline won't sag open. Press the band and the sweater together.

Topstitch around the edging, leaving the last half-inch—where the binding meets itself—unstitched. Unpin and press.

Repin the binding to the outside, and press it again. Topstitch the binding around the outside, leaving the last bit unstitched.

Unravel both ends of the binding until they don't quite meet. The binding will look better if it is pulled a little tight. Graft the two ends together so the band looks like a continuous circle.

Around the hem. Decide how wide you want the band to be. Knit a strip twice that wide, because it will be folded over. Because the band won't stretch, measure accurately for the hem edge, and knit the band to that length. Full and press the band.

Gather or ease the sweater onto the band, on the inside of the sweater. Pin and press it in place, then topstitch the band onto the inside.

Take out the pins and fold the band in half to the outside. Pin and press it, then topstitch it to the outside, leaving the last half-inch unstitched.

Unravel both ends until they gap a little, then graft them together. Press the graft until it's invisible. Press the hem edging until it resembles an act of God.

Around the sleeve. Decide how wide you want the band, and knit it twice that width so you can fold it in half. Measure around your fist to see how long to make it, because it won't stretch. You probably won't make a fist when you put on your clothes, but this amount of band will permit easy dressing under normal conditions.

Knit two bands, each as long as the circumference of your fist. Full and press them. Gather or ease the sleeve onto the cuff band, using plenty of pins to even the easing. Press the band and the cuff.

Sew the bands in place as you would a hem band, first the inside and then the outside. Graft the ravellies until the join is invisible, and press when the sewing is done.

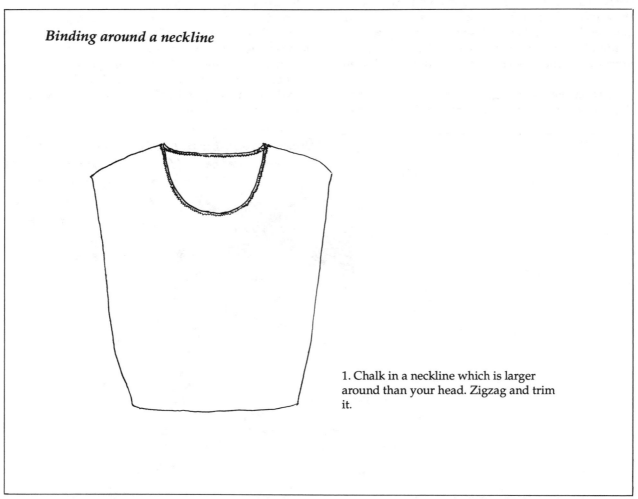

Binding around a neckline

1. Chalk in a neckline which is larger around than your head. Zigzag and trim it.

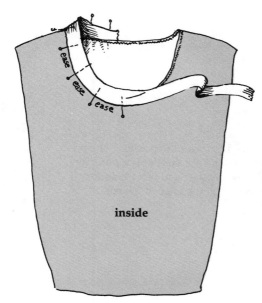

inside

2. Make an edging band between 1½" and 2" wide. Pin it to the inside neckline. The band should just cover the zigzagging. Ease the sweater onto the band, or else the neckline will be floppy. Press band and sweater together, and topstitch at the edge of the band.

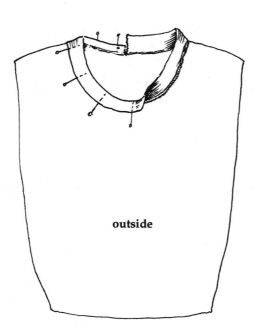

outside

3. Fold the band to the outside. Press it smooth, and topstitch it.

4. Unravel the ends of the binding piece and graft them together.

Binding around a hem

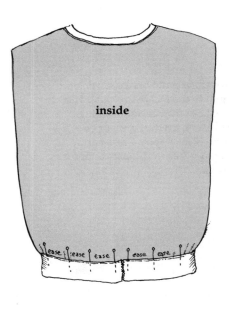

inside

1. Pin an edging band to the inside hem of the sweater. Ease the sweater onto the band. Press sweater and band together, and topstitch at the edge of the band.

2. Fold the band to the outside. Pin and press it. Topstitch at the edge of the band.

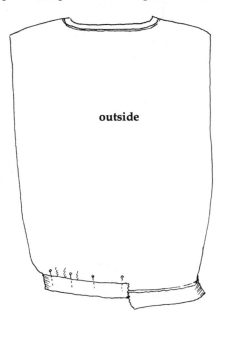

outside

3. Unravel both ends of the band and graft them together.

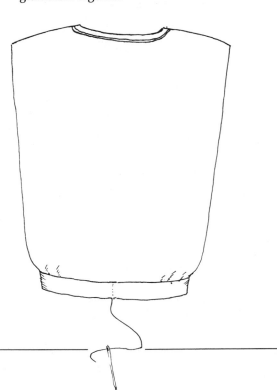

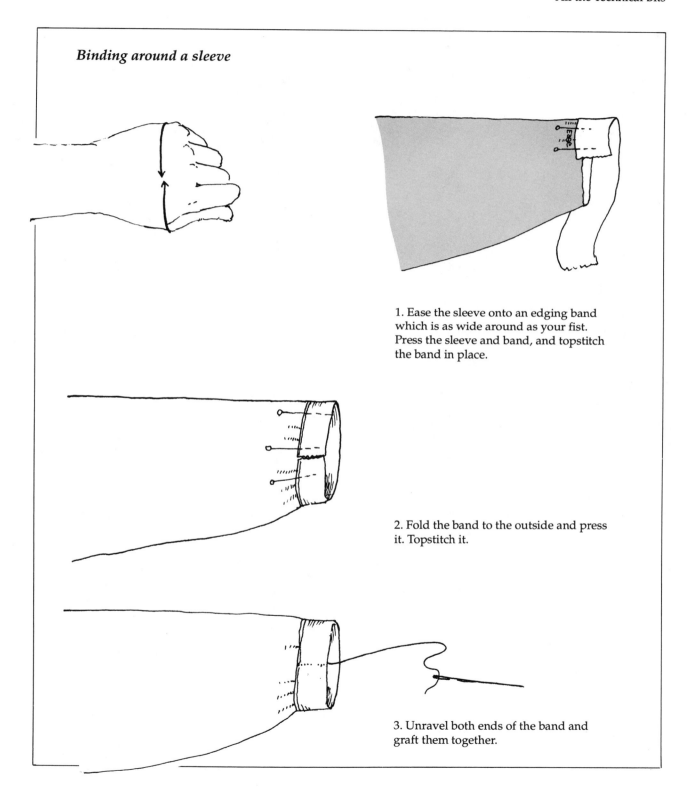

Binding around a sleeve

1. Ease the sleeve onto an edging band which is as wide around as your fist. Press the sleeve and band, and topstitch the band in place.

2. Fold the band to the outside and press it. Topstitch it.

3. Unravel both ends of the band and graft them together.

Drop-Shoulder Sweaters

cartwright-jones

Drop-shoulder sweaters

Drop-shoulder sweaters get their name because the shoulder seam drops down somewhere toward your bicep. This always makes the sweater look nonchalant and cozy. There is no shaping to do at the top of the sleeve—it's straight across. There's no armhole shaping on the body piece—it's mostly straight up and down. Folk knitters in many lands have made drop-shoulder sweaters for generations for these reasons. They are blessedly, beautifully simple.

The straightforward construction invites the use of pattern, texture, or intriguing yarns. If you want to plan a design that travels all the way around the front, back, and sleeves, remember that when the sweater is worn the top of the sleeve lies about 8" below the top of the body.

Some drop-shoulder sweaters fit poorly under the armpits because their shoulder seams go straight across while the wearer's shoulders slope. To avoid this problem, you can half-fashion a sloping shoulder seam. You will also need to choose a neckline type and half-fashion it.

Design. First, sketch your ideas for your sweater. Pencil in different necklines and maybe patterns. If you're working with several colors, try crayons. You'll avoid some ripping out later if you do extra sketching and erasing now. If you like the garment on paper, you'll like it knitted up. Granted, there

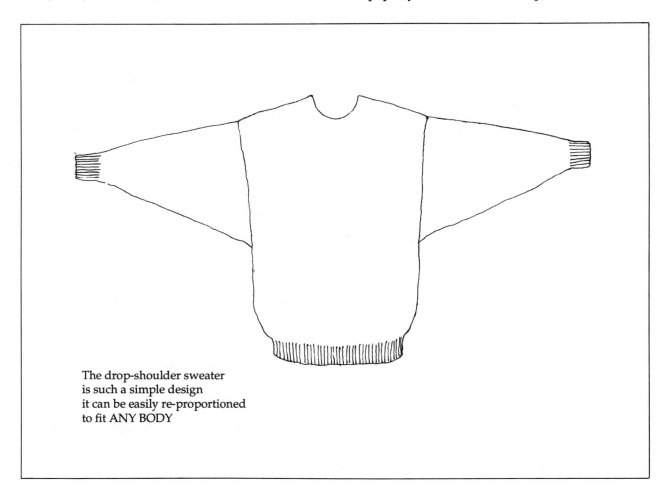

The drop-shoulder sweater
is such a simple design
it can be easily re-proportioned
to fit ANY BODY

are always surprises, but if you plan ahead they won't be tragic. Get out the swatch you think has the best sweater potential, knit a gauge-sized swatch, and full it.

Measure. When you've drawn your sweater, measure your chest, hips, arms, head, neck, and the length of the sweater. If you've forgotten how to do this, look back at pages 16–17.

Decide how loose you want the sweater. Widening the body will decrease the sleeve length; some people think they want voluminous sweaters until they notice that their shoulder seams have dropped to their elbows, and their sleeves aren't much longer than their cuffs.

Calculate. Write your measurements on the calculation pages (page 78). Figure out the body first. The two body pieces will be rectangles, or they will widen out a bit from the bottom up. Because a person's arm measurement begins at the nape of the neck, the sweater's arm measurement begins at its center line. Subtract half of the width of the body from the arm length; the remainder is the sleeve length.

Draft. When you've written in your measurements, multiply each by the gauge from your swatch to change inches into stitches and rows. If you've forgotten how to do this, see page 14. Write your stitch and row counts on the draft page (page 79); this is your sweater pattern.

Knit. Pin up your design and your draft, side by side, next to your knitting machine. Knit the sweater, using the draft as a road map and your design as a travel guide.

Knit the neckline you have decided on.

How do you want the sweater to fit?

Slim fit
Add 0" to chest
Add 0" to hip

Cozy fit
Add 3" to chest
Add 2" to hip

Loose fit
Add 6" to chest
Add 4" to hip

Very loose fit
Add 9" to chest
Add 6" to hip

Gorilla fit
Add 12" to chest
Add 8" to hip

Full the sweater pieces, give them a good pressing, and hook up any dropped stitches. Fix anything else that needs it.

Measure the pieces, to see if they came out close to your calculations. If something's unreasonably long, unravel. If something's peculiarly short, rehang it and add a few rows. Is it all right now?

Sew. Join the front and back, half-fashioning the shoulders. The shoulder usually slopes down 1" for every 3" it travels across. The neck opening is usually 8" across—check back in the technical department under necklines for more information.

If these dimensions seem way off, by all means take some extra measurements and chalk in what will fit.

Sew in your neckline finish or collar, and then press the seams with a lot of steam. Zigzag across the tops of the sleeves, so they won't unravel, stretching them out slightly as you zigzag. Match the centers of the sleeve tops to the shoulder seams. Stretch the sleeves slightly as you iron and pin them into place; this makes the armpits a bit more comfortable. Sew the sleeves to the body, and press the seam smooth.

Sew up the side seams. Press, steam, press, and steam every seam and expanse of fabric until the sweater looks like Zeus himself breathed it into existence.

Put your sweater on and admire yourself for a while. Looks pretty good, eh?

Measurements for a drop-shoulder sweater
(See pages 16–19 for how to measure, and page 73 for notes on ease.)

	Body	Adjustment (for ease, cutting, and seams)	Adjusted measurement
Chest	____ "	+ 0–12" ease	____ "
Hips	____ "	+ 0–12" ease	____ "
Wrist	____ "	+ 3"	____ "
Arm length	____ "		
Sweater length	____ "	+ 3" for cutting & seams	____ "
Other	____ "		____ "
	____ "		____ "
	____ "		____ "

Will you want to work increases on the front and back?

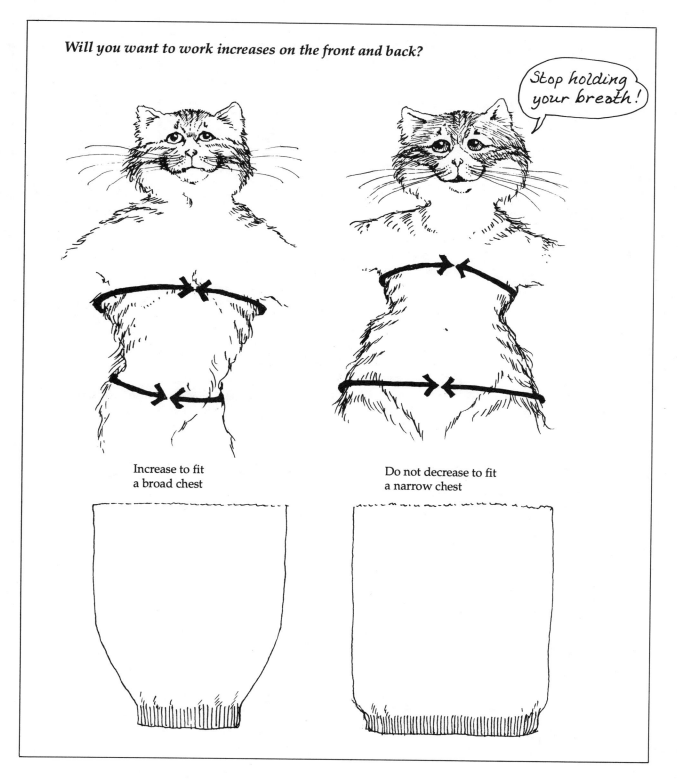

Increase to fit
a broad chest

Do not decrease to fit
a narrow chest

Design a drop-shoulder sweater

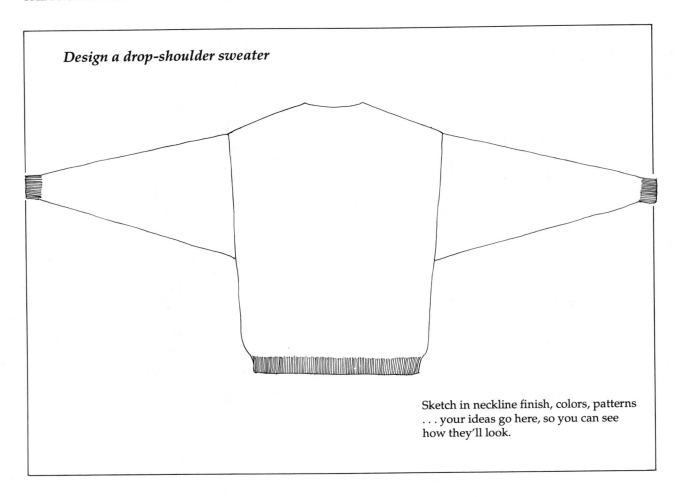

Sketch in neckline finish, colors, patterns
. . . your ideas go here, so you can see
how they'll look.

Figure out your drop-shoulder sweater

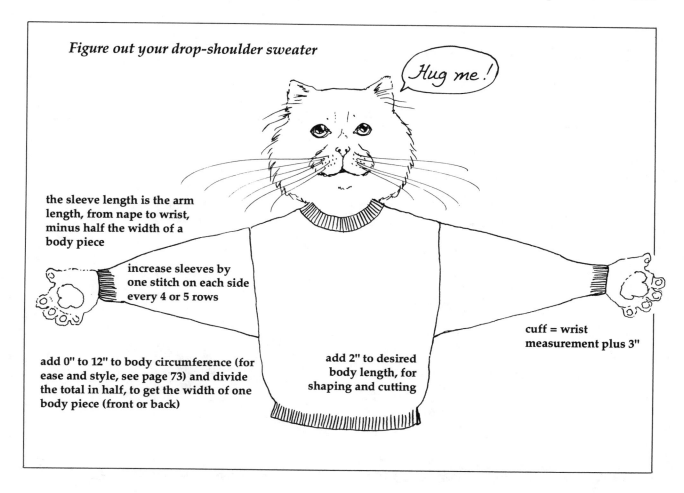

the sleeve length is the arm length, from nape to wrist, minus half the width of a body piece

increase sleeves by one stitch on each side every 4 or 5 rows

cuff = wrist measurement plus 3"

add 0" to 12" to body circumference (for ease and style, see page 73) and divide the total in half, to get the width of one body piece (front or back)

add 2" to desired body length, for shaping and cutting

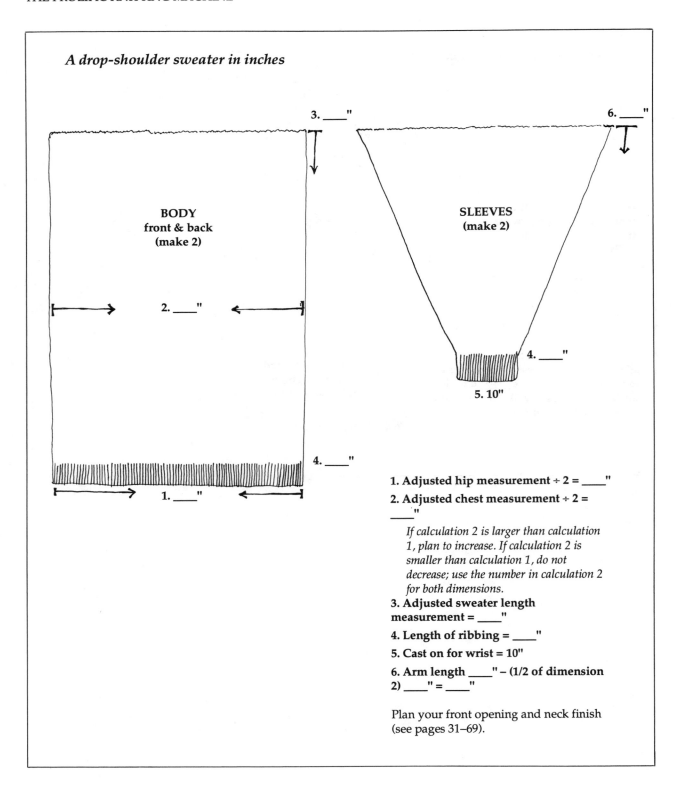

A drop-shoulder sweater in inches

3. ____"

6. ____"

BODY
front & back
(make 2)

SLEEVES
(make 2)

2. ____"

4. ____"

5. 10"

4. ____"

1. ____"

1. **Adjusted hip measurement ÷ 2 = ____"**

2. **Adjusted chest measurement ÷ 2 = ____"**

If calculation 2 is larger than calculation 1, plan to increase. If calculation 2 is smaller than calculation 1, do not decrease; use the number in calculation 2 for both dimensions.

3. **Adjusted sweater length measurement = ____"**

4. **Length of ribbing = ____"**

5. **Cast on for wrist = 10"**

6. **Arm length ____" – (1/2 of dimension 2) ____" = ____"**

Plan your front opening and neck finish (see pages 31–69).

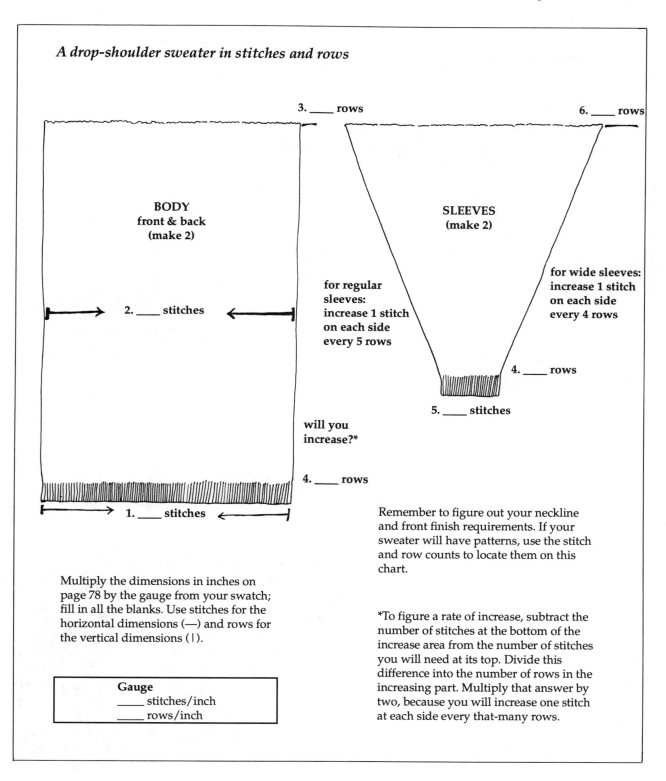

A drop-shoulder sweater in stitches and rows

3. ____ rows

6. ____ rows

BODY
front & back
(make 2)

SLEEVES
(make 2)

2. ____ stitches

**for regular
sleeves:
increase 1 stitch
on each side
every 5 rows**

**for wide sleeves:
increase 1 stitch
on each side
every 4 rows**

4. ____ rows

5. ____ stitches

**will you
increase?***

4. ____ rows

1. ____ stitches

Remember to figure out your neckline
and front finish requirements. If your
sweater will have patterns, use the stitch
and row counts to locate them on this
chart.

Multiply the dimensions in inches on
page 78 by the gauge from your swatch;
fill in all the blanks. Use stitches for the
horizontal dimensions (—) and rows for
the vertical dimensions (|).

*To figure a rate of increase, subtract the
number of stitches at the bottom of the
increase area from the number of stitches
you will need at its top. Divide this
difference into the number of rows in the
increasing part. Multiply that answer by
two, because you will increase one stitch
at each side every that-many rows.

Gauge
____ stitches/inch
____ rows/inch

Putting together a drop-shoulder sweater

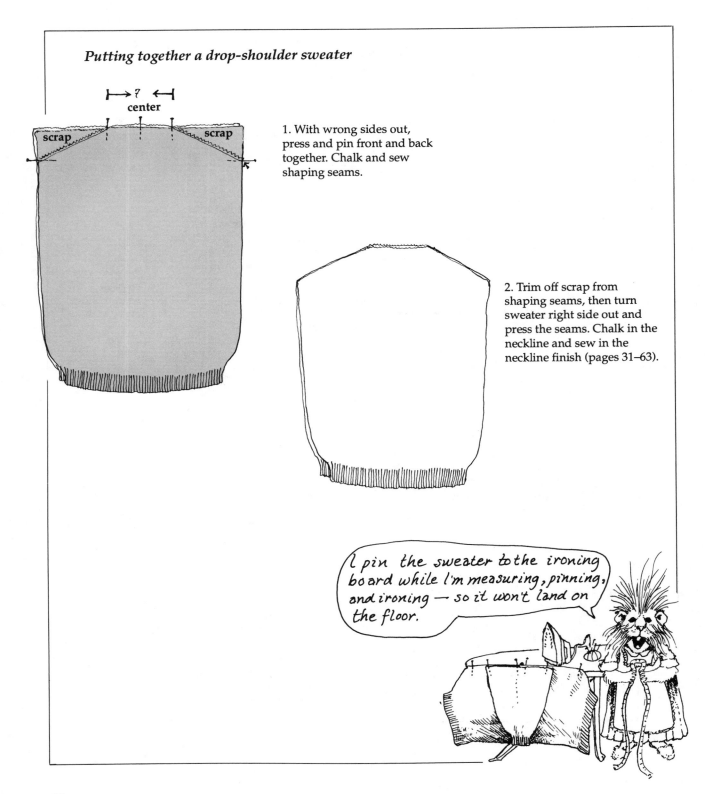

1. With wrong sides out, press and pin front and back together. Chalk and sew shaping seams.

2. Trim off scrap from shaping seams, then turn sweater right side out and press the seams. Chalk in the neckline and sew in the neckline finish (pages 31–63).

I pin the sweater to the ironing board while I'm measuring, pinning, and ironing — so it won't land on the floor.

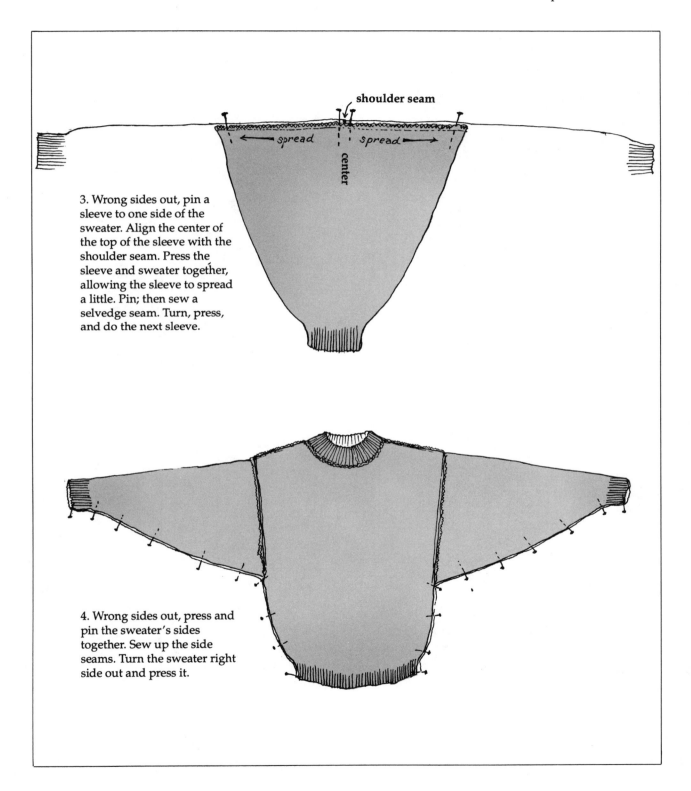

shoulder seam

spread   *spread*

center

3. Wrong sides out, pin a sleeve to one side of the sweater. Align the center of the top of the sleeve with the shoulder seam. Press the sleeve and sweater together, allowing the sleeve to spread a little. Pin; then sew a selvedge seam. Turn, press, and do the next sleeve.

4. Wrong sides out, press and pin the sweater's sides together. Sew up the side seams. Turn the sweater right side out and press it.

Raglan Sweaters

Raglan sweaters

Raglan sweaters have a yoke that invites wonderful patterning around the shoulders. The generous sleeves and low armpits on these sweaters are very comfortable, and they hang a little more gracefully than drop-shoulder sweaters.

If a sweater is beautiful and comfortable, let it also be simple. Beauty dies horribly when burdened with too many instructions. Raglans can be simple: draft one yoke for front, back, and both sleeves. This is not only easy to calculate, but your patterning will match up all around.

Draft and calculate the yoke. Pick out your best potential sample and knit a gauge swatch. Figure out your gauge first, because you'll need the numbers to figure the yoke. Get your chest measurement, too, add ease in inches (see page 73), and divide the number in half because you'll need to know the width of the front body piece right away.

The yoke is a trapezoid, and it is drafted as follows. The top of the trapezoid will be 6" across. How many stitches is that at your gauge? The bottom of the trapezoid will be 20" or the width of the front of the sweater, whichever is smaller. How many stitches is that at your gauge? Subtract the number of stitches at the top from the number of stitches at the bottom. That is the number of rows from the bottom to the top of the yoke.

You will decrease two stitches on each side every fourth row (or one stitch on each side every other row), from the bottom of the yoke to the top. That's the yoke shaping for the front, back, and both sleeves. Unless you're working on a bulky machine with thick yarn, use the two-eyed tool and the first shaping technique so you don't have to stop so often.

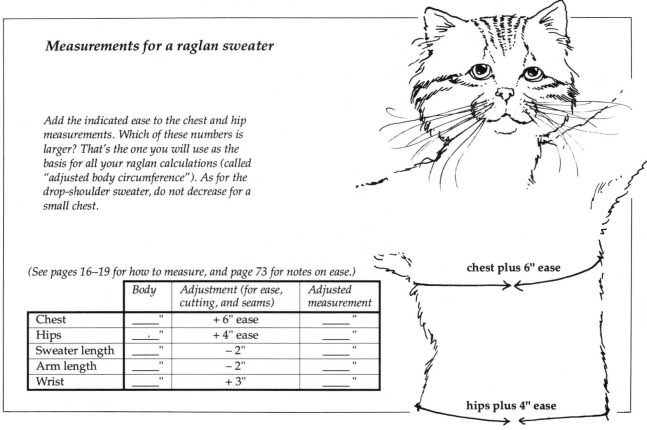

Measurements for a raglan sweater

Add the indicated ease to the chest and hip measurements. Which of these numbers is larger? That's the one you will use as the basis for all your raglan calculations (called "adjusted body circumference"). As for the drop-shoulder sweater, do not decrease for a small chest.

(See pages 16–19 for how to measure, and page 73 for notes on ease.)

	Body	Adjustment (for ease, cutting, and seams)	Adjusted measurement
Chest	_____"	+ 6" ease	_____"
Hips	_____"	+ 4" ease	_____"
Sweater length	_____"	− 2"	_____"
Arm length	_____"	− 2"	_____"
Wrist	_____"	+ 3"	_____"

chest plus 6" ease

hips plus 4" ease

Figure out the top and bottom dimensions of the yoke

The underarm-to-neckline section of a raglan sweater is called the yoke. The way I make raglans, the underarm-to-neckline sections of front, back, and both sleeves are constructed exactly the same, so one set of figures is all you need.

The top dimension of any raglan yoke is 6". Calculate the bottom dimension as follows:

Divide the adjusted body circumference (_____") by 2 = _____".
This is the measurement of the yoke at its bottom edge.

Up to 40" adjusted body circumference

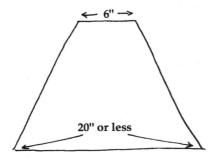

If the yoke's bottom dimension is 20" or less, the yoke will look like this.

Over 40" adjusted body circumference

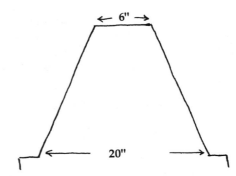

If the yoke's bottom dimension is more than 20", bind off the extra inches at the bottom, half on each side, so the yoke is 20" across at the point where you start to decrease.

Using your gauge numbers, translate inches into stitches.

Gauge
_____ stitches/inch
_____ rows/inch

How many stitches will you need to bind off to reduce the bottom width of the yoke to 20"?

Front and back. How long should the sweater be? Subtract 2" from the desired length (which was measured with a great sigh), because the yoke starts about 2" down from the shoulderline. How many rows is that? Subtract the rows of the yoke from this total number of rows for the body. You now have the number of the row on which you will begin the yoke decreasing.

How wide should the body be? Add 4" and 6" to the hip and chest measurements, respectively. Divide these numbers in half, for front and back widths. If the width of the sweater front or back at the chest is more than 20", cast off enough stitches at each side on the first yoke row to reduce the width to 20".

Sleeves. How long should the sleeves be? Measure from the nape of the neck over the shoulder to the wrist. Subtract 2", because the raglan sleeve stops at the neck. How many rows is that? Subtract the rows of the yoke from the rows of the sleeve. You now have the number of the row on which you begin yoke decreases for the sleeves.

Between the cuff and the yoke decrease, you will have to increase the sleeve to the same width as the front and back. How many stitches wide is your cuff? (It will measure about 10".) How many stitches wide was the body at the chest? Subtract the number of cuff stitches from the number of chest stitches. This is the number of stitches you will need to increase on each sleeve.

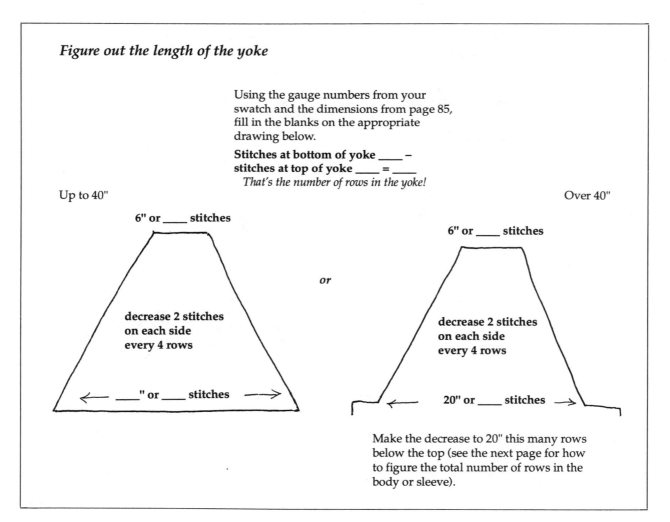

Figure out the length of the yoke

Using the gauge numbers from your swatch and the dimensions from page 85, fill in the blanks on the appropriate drawing below.

**Stitches at bottom of yoke _____ –
stitches at top of yoke _____ = _____**
That's the number of rows in the yoke!

Up to 40"

6" or _____ stitches

decrease 2 stitches
on each side
every 4 rows

←—— _____" or _____ stitches ——→

or

Over 40"

6" or _____ stitches

decrease 2 stitches
on each side
every 4 rows

←—— 20" or _____ stitches ——→

Make the decrease to 20" this many rows below the top (see the next page for how to figure the total number of rows in the body or sleeve).

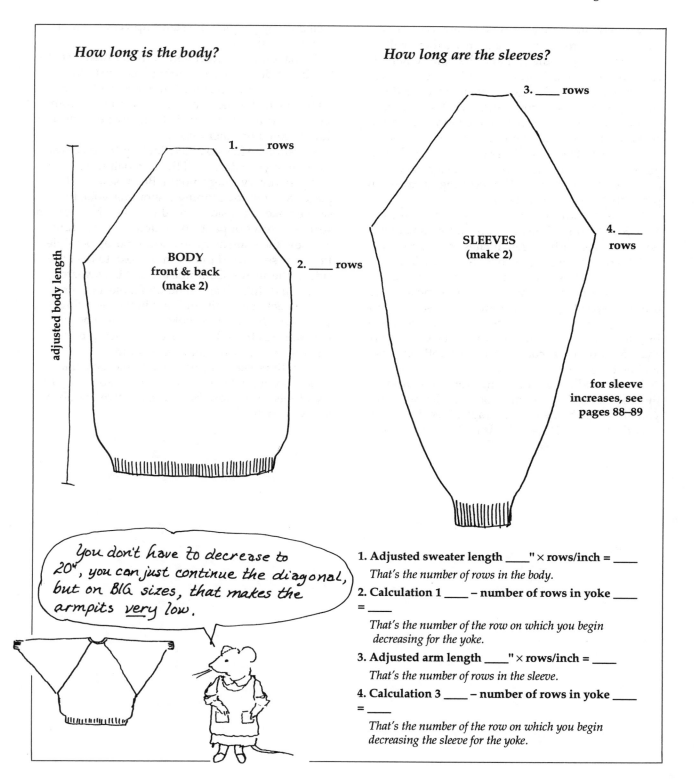

How long is the body?

How long are the sleeves?

3. ____ rows

1. ____ rows

BODY
front & back
(make 2)

2. ____ rows

adjusted body length

SLEEVES
(make 2)

4. ____
rows

for sleeve
increases, see
pages 88–89

You don't have to decrease to 20″, you can just continue the diagonal, but on BIG sizes, that makes the armpits very low.

1. **Adjusted sweater length ____″ × rows/inch = ____**
   That's the number of rows in the body.

2. **Calculation 1 ____ – number of rows in yoke ____**
   = ____
   That's the number of the row on which you begin decreasing for the yoke.

3. **Adjusted arm length ____″ × rows/inch = ____**
   That's the number of rows in the sleeve.

4. **Calculation 3 ____ – number of rows in yoke ____**
   = ____
   That's the number of the row on which you begin decreasing the sleeve for the yoke.

Now you need to determine where to place the increases. Figure out how many rows there will be between the top of the cuff and the point where the yoke decreases will begin by multiplying the length of the sleeve, from top of cuff to yoke-decrease point, by your row gauge. That's the number of rows you will have in which to work your increases. Divide the total number of rows by the number of stitches to be increased and double that number, since every time you increase you will add a stitch at each side. The resulting number will probably be between 3 and 4.

Unless the number you came up with was exactly 3 or 4, you will need to do a little adjusting when you get within a few inches of the row on which you will begin the yoke decreases. Your sleeve needs to be exactly as wide as each body piece at that point. Within the last few inches, slow down or speed up the rate of increases so this happens; this "tweaking" will be minor. See the drawings for details. As you work the first sleeve, keep track of how you accomplish this so both sleeves will be the same.

What neckline do you want? You can simply rib the last 1½" of the yoke and cast off. That will give you an old-fashioned square raglan neckline. The only drawback to this finish is that it can be worn well only by people who stand up very straight and do not slouch.

Prepare for any other sort of neck finish by continuing to decrease the knitting past the 6" top width point; add an extra 2" of fabric and drop it off unfinished. When you have sewn up the four shoulder seams, you can chalk in any neckline and add its collar or other finish.

Finishing. After you have knit up the pieces according to your draft, full them, repair the glitches, and press everything smooth. Begin sewing the pieces together by pinning a shoulder yoke to a sleeve yoke, right sides together. If you have put in stripes or rows of patterns, match them carefully and sew the seam as close to the edge as possible. Press the seam, and pin the next yoke to the other side of the sleeve. Continue around the sweater.

If you didn't rib and bind off an old-fashioned raglan neckline, chalk and sew in the neck finish you want after the four yoke seams have been joined. Press the sides and sleeves, then pin them together and sew the underarm seams.

Turn the sweater right side out and give it a good, thorough pressing. Try it on. A good raglan sweater is so comfortable and attractive, it's absolutely seductive!

How to place the sleeve increases

For each sleeve, you will cast on enough stitches to comfortably fit around the wrist (see pages 93–94). By the time you reach the underarm and begin the yoke decreases, the sleeves will need to be the same width as the body sections. The rate-of-increase for your raglan sleeves may not be an even number, but it will be between 3 and 4 (see description at left).

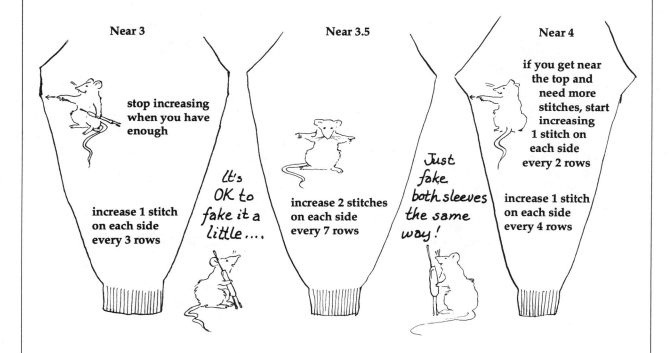

Near 3

stop increasing when you have enough

increase 1 stitch on each side every 3 rows

It's OK to fake it a little....

Near 3.5

increase 2 stitches on each side every 7 rows

Just fake both sleeves the same way!

Near 4

if you get near the top and need more stitches, start increasing 1 stitch on each side every 2 rows

increase 1 stitch on each side every 4 rows

If your increase number is near 3, for example 3.21469, increase 1 stitch on each side every 3 rows. Stop increasing when the sleeve is wide enough.

If your increase number is near 3.5, for example 3.45 or 3.63, increase 2 stitches on each side every 7 rows. Stop increasing when the sleeve is wide enough (see "near 3") or work additional increases as you approach the top (see "near 4"), as needed.

If your increase number is near 4, for example 3.85, increase 1 stitch on each side every 4 rows to begin. When you reach the top and need extra stitches, increase 1 stitch on each side every 2 rows.

Two types of raglan necklines

Squared raglan necklines are old-fashioned classics, but they only gracefully fit people who stand very straight. They are the same depth in front and in back.

Most people don't stand up straight, so a half-fashioned neckline will fit them better. This neckline is higher in back and lower in front.

 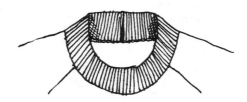

Make this collar by ribbing the last 1½" of each yoke piece, and binding off at the row in which the yoke becomes 6" wide.

Knit 2" extra on each yoke section, still decreasing, past the row on which the yoke becomes 6" wide. Chalk in a neckline and half-fashion a separately knitted neckline finish.

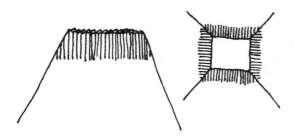 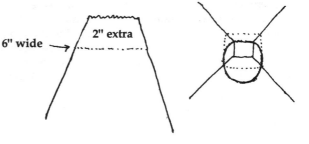

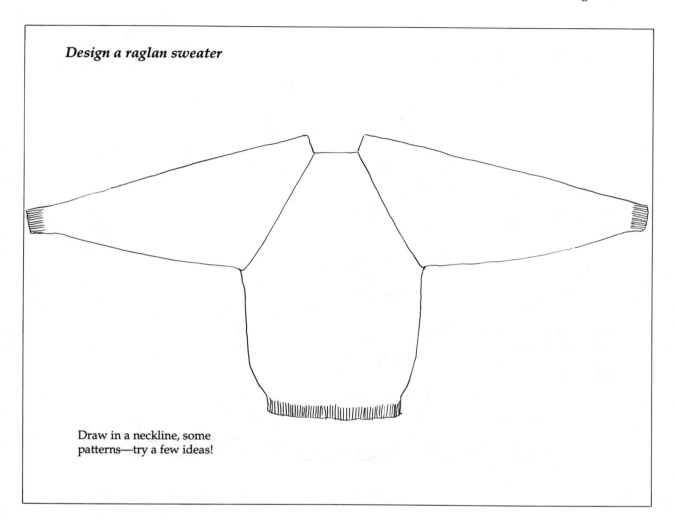

Design a raglan sweater

Draw in a neckline, some
patterns—try a few ideas!

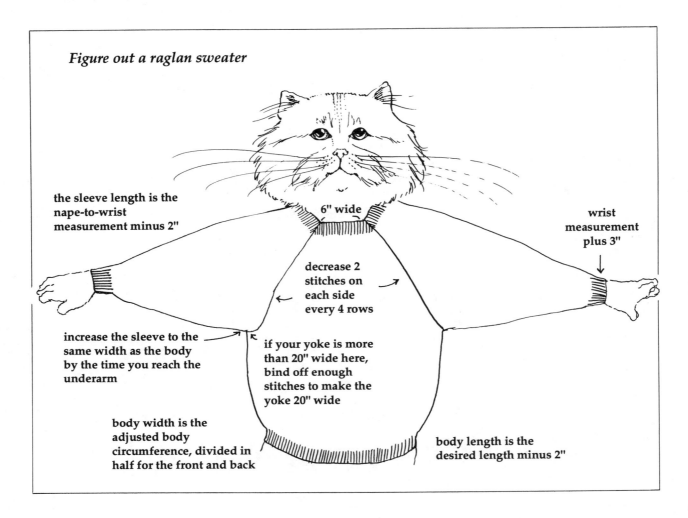

Figure out a raglan sweater

6" wide

the sleeve length is the nape-to-wrist measurement minus 2"

wrist measurement plus 3"

decrease 2 stitches on each side every 4 rows

increase the sleeve to the same width as the body by the time you reach the underarm

if your yoke is more than 20" wide here, bind off enough stitches to make the yoke 20" wide

body width is the adjusted body circumference, divided in half for the front and back

body length is the desired length minus 2"

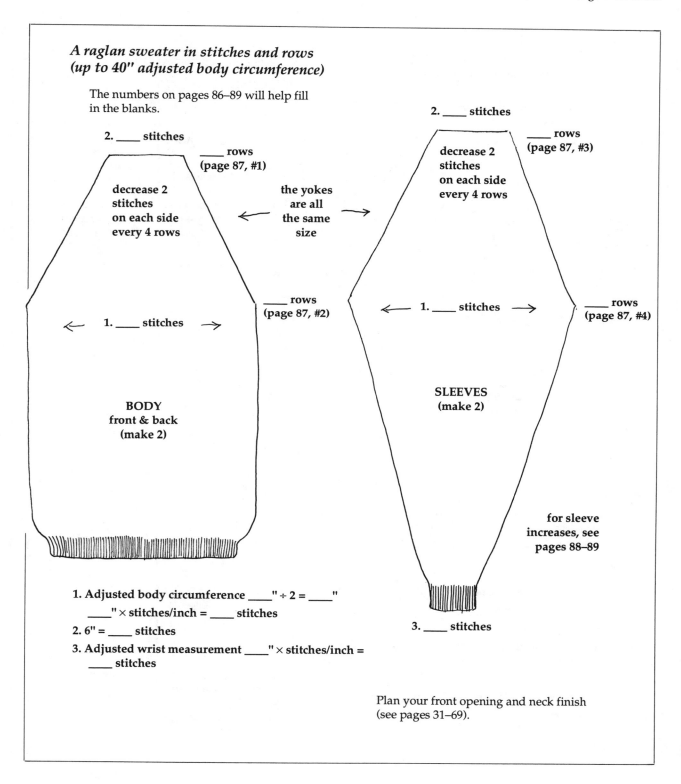

A raglan sweater in stitches and rows (up to 40" adjusted body circumference)

The numbers on pages 86–89 will help fill in the blanks.

2. ____ stitches

____ rows (page 87, #1)

decrease 2 stitches on each side every 4 rows

← the yokes are all the same size →

1. ____ stitches

____ rows (page 87, #2)

BODY front & back (make 2)

2. ____ stitches

____ rows (page 87, #3)

decrease 2 stitches on each side every 4 rows

1. ____ stitches

____ rows (page 87, #4)

SLEEVES (make 2)

for sleeve increases, see pages 88–89

3. ____ stitches

1. Adjusted body circumference ____" ÷ 2 = ____"
____" × stitches/inch = ____ stitches

2. 6" = ____ stitches

3. Adjusted wrist measurement ____" × stitches/inch = ____ stitches

Plan your front opening and neck finish (see pages 31–69).

93

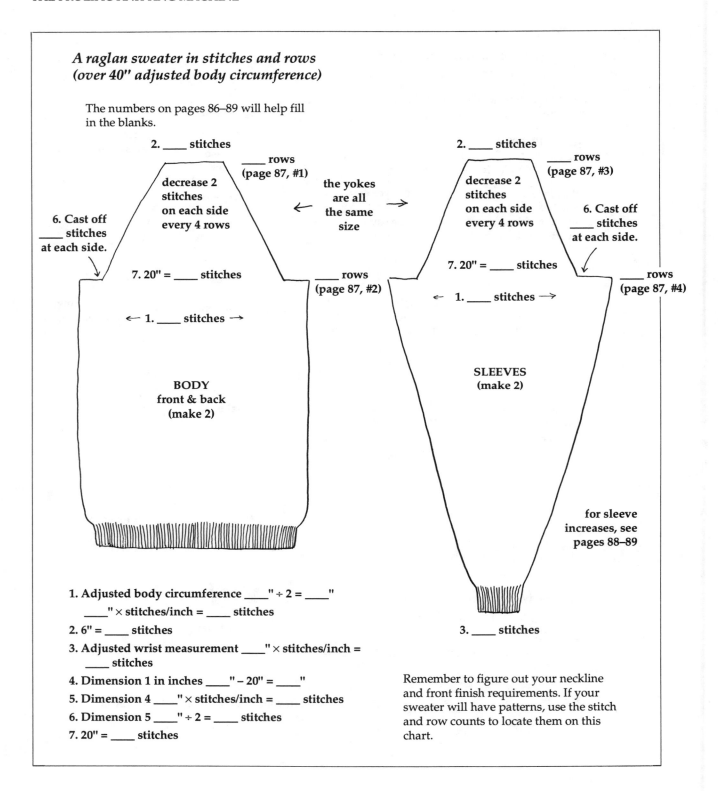

A raglan sweater in stitches and rows (over 40" adjusted body circumference)

The numbers on pages 86–89 will help fill in the blanks.

2. ____ stitches

____ rows (page 87, #1)

decrease 2 stitches on each side every 4 rows

the yokes are all the same size

6. Cast off ____ stitches at each side.

7. 20" = ____ stitches

____ rows (page 87, #2)

← 1. ____ stitches →

BODY
front & back
(make 2)

2. ____ stitches

____ rows (page 87, #3)

decrease 2 stitches on each side every 4 rows

6. Cast off ____ stitches at each side.

7. 20" = ____ stitches

1. ____ stitches →

____ rows (page 87, #4)

SLEEVES
(make 2)

for sleeve increases, see pages 88–89

1. Adjusted body circumference ____" ÷ 2 = ____"
   ____" × stitches/inch = ____ stitches

2. 6" = ____ stitches

3. Adjusted wrist measurement ____" × stitches/inch = ____ stitches

4. Dimension 1 in inches ____" – 20" = ____"

5. Dimension 4 ____" × stitches/inch = ____ stitches

6. Dimension 5 ____" ÷ 2 = ____ stitches

7. 20" = ____ stitches

3. ____ stitches

Remember to figure out your neckline and front finish requirements. If your sweater will have patterns, use the stitch and row counts to locate them on this chart.

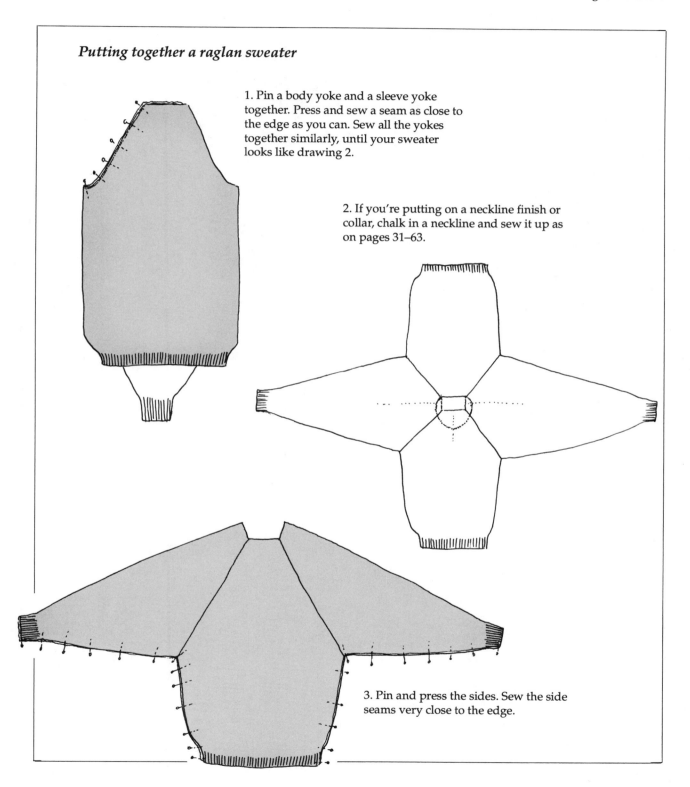

Putting together a raglan sweater

1. Pin a body yoke and a sleeve yoke together. Press and sew a seam as close to the edge as you can. Sew all the yokes together similarly, until your sweater looks like drawing 2.

2. If you're putting on a neckline finish or collar, chalk in a neckline and sew it up as on pages 31–63.

3. Pin and press the sides. Sew the side seams very close to the edge.

English-Style Vests

English-style vests

English-style vests fit closely, have ribbing at the armholes, and often sport V-necks and Fair Isle patterning. They are indispensable in British television series about cozy middle-class chaps, especially if the chaps are rural or eccentric. A perfectly fitted English vest is a great compromise between a suit vest and a sweater. It hasn't the pretensions of a suit, nor is it as decidedly sporty as a sweater. A knitted vest may pass in an office where a sweater never would, and is welcome on days which require a bit of coziness. If a vest fits beautifully, it's a joy to wear; if it fits badly, it will be worn only when digging root crops.

Measure. Measurements for a vest must be more exact than for a sweater, and there are more of them. When in doubt, take more measurements rather than fewer, particularly if the vest is for an extraordinary body. If the vest is for you, you may want to have someone else take the measurements.

Point to where the bottom edge of the vest should be. Measure from the shoulder seam of the shirt to that hemline. Then, while still holding the tape measure in place, stretch and yawn, or have your subject do so. That should add 3" to the length, and will give you the correct length for the vest. A vest should be long enough to blouse a little when you stand at rest, and to resist pulling up when you reach for something.

People with very big bellies should have their lengths measured with the tape held near center front, so the greatest longitude is accounted for. People with scoliosis may need an extra back measurement.

Measure around your chest, with your arms out a bit, at what seems to be the widest place.

Measure around your middle—a little above navel level is a waist.

Measure the circumference at the point where you want the bottom edge of your vest.

If you're wearing a shirt with sleeves, measure down from the apex (tiptop) of your shoulder to an inch below the armpit seam. The vest's armhole must not crumple a shirtsleeve, and there will be ribbing—1½" to 2" of it—added. If you're not wearing such a convenient garment, the very tickly spot

a few ribs below your armpit is a good spot to measure to.

Point to where the bottom of the V-neck opening should be. Measure from the shoulder seam down to that place. If you're using a V-neck, or any other sort of neck finish, refer back to pages 31–45 for particulars.

Measure from the outer edge of one shoulder to the outer edge of the other. Whew.

Design. Work out your ideas, pull out all of your favorite swatches, draw the vest the way you want it. If you're indulging in Fair Isle work, figure out how many rows your patterns require.

Calculate. Write in all the measurements. Vests need to fit smoothly, so don't add more than 3" to any latitude.

Draft. Get your gauge from your swatch. Multiply all the measurements on the calculations page by stitches and rows. To figure out how much ribbing you'll need for the neck and armhole bands, pull on the ribbing of the swatch and calculate from the stretched-out gauge. Vest ribbing is sewn stretched, so it will not stick out like little wings on your shoulders and wrinkle up under your arms.

If you're doing Fair Isle, add row numbers for starting the patterns to the draft.

Knit. Pin your design where you can see it, for inspiration, and the draft next to it, for a road map. When you get to the armpit, where you need to narrow the vest, don't bother casting off. Just drop the appropriate needles back out of the knitting, and let the corners curl back. You don't need to zigzag these edges before fulling, either.

Full. Full your vest the way your favorite sample swatch was fulled. Press all the pieces and measure them to see if they match the calculations sheet. Chalk, zigzag, and cut them to size if they came out big, or rehang and knit a little more if they're small.

Sew. Zigzag the upper edges of the vest. Sew the front and back together across the top. Chalk a little arc where each armpit cut is to be, and zigzag each arc. Trim off the extra fabric. Chalk and proceed with your neckline as described on pages 31–45. Give everything a good pressing.

Figure out a vest

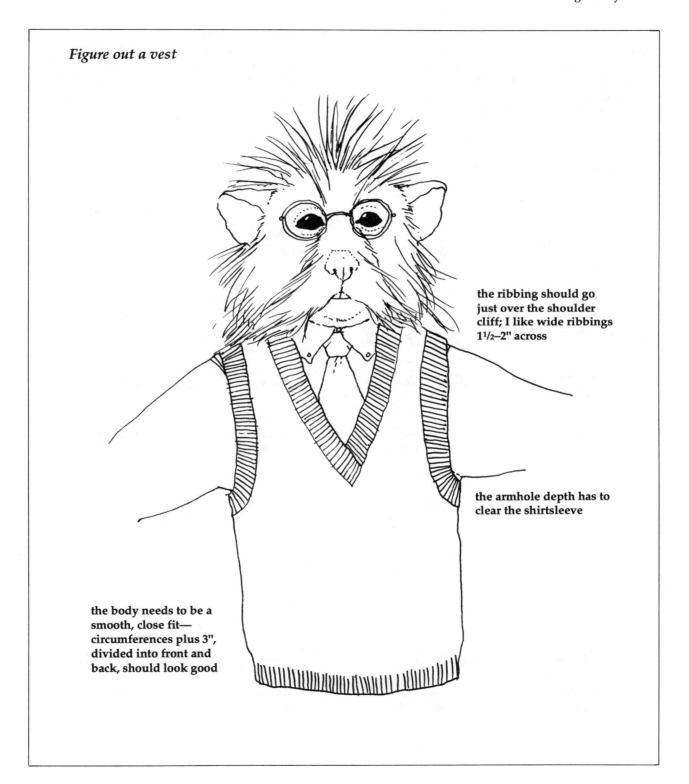

the ribbing should go just over the shoulder cliff; I like wide ribbings 1½–2" across

the armhole depth has to clear the shirtsleeve

the body needs to be a smooth, close fit—circumferences plus 3", divided into front and back, should look good

Zigzag your armhole ribbing, stretching each piece out wide as you sew. Pin each ribbing piece in place. Give the ribbings an extra pressing before you sew them on, and stretch body and ribbing to meet smoothly as you sew. Keep your seam as narrow as you can. Press the finished seams with all the steam you can muster.

Sew the side seams, keeping them as narrow as possible. Steam and press all that again, stretching the armhole ribbing over the narrow curve of your ironing board and steaming away until the ribbing looks just right.

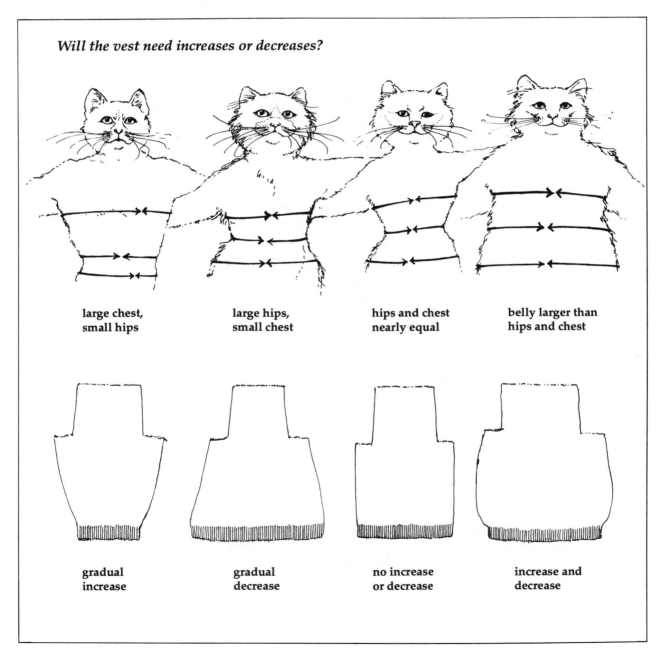

Will the vest need increases or decreases?

large chest, small hips

large hips, small chest

hips and chest nearly equal

belly larger than hips and chest

gradual increase

gradual decrease

no increase or decrease

increase and decrease

If the ribbing puckers up your vest, mist the recalcitrant areas with a spray of water, and hang knitting weights at the pucker points (if you don't have enough weights, little pouches of pennies hung on Christmas hooks do the job).

If the ribbing is floppy—a common plague of cotton and silk—thread some elastic through the back side of the ribbing.

The vest should be done and looking good now. Try it on. Perfect, isn't it? Go collect some admiring glances at a pub.

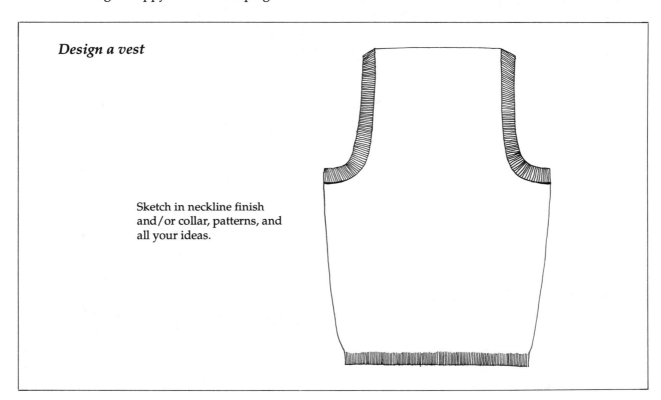

Design a vest

Sketch in neckline finish and/or collar, patterns, and all your ideas.

Measurements for a vest
(See pages 16–19 for how to measure.)

	Body	Adjustment (for ease, cutting, and seams)	Adjusted measurement
Chest	___ "	+ 3"	___ "
Waist	___ "	+ 3"	___ "
Hips	___ "	+ 3"	___ "
Shoulders	___ "		
Armhole depth	___ "		
Vest length	___ "	+ 1" for cutting & seams	___ "

Plan a decrease in the body if the hips are larger than the chest. Plan an increase in the body if the chest is larger than the hips. Do not decrease for a small waist.

A vest in inches

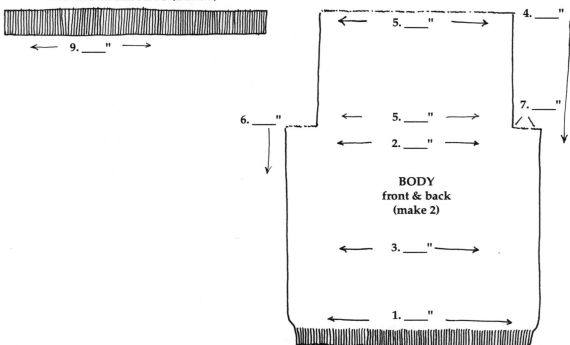

ARMHOLE RIBBING (make 2)

9. ____"

4. ____"

5. ____"

6. ____"

7. ____"

5. ____"

2. ____"

BODY
front & back
(make 2)

3. ____"

1. ____"

1. **Adjusted hip measurement** ____" ÷ 2 = ____"

2. **Adjusted chest measurement** ____" ÷ 2 = ____"

3. **Adjusted waist measurement** ____" ÷ 2 = ____"

If hips are larger than chest, plan a decrease. If chest is larger than hips, plan an increase. If waist is largest, plan to increase and then decrease. Do not decrease for a small waist.

4. **Adjusted vest length measurement** ____" = ____"

5. **Shoulders** ____" – 4" = ____"

6. **Dimension 4** ____" – armhole depth ____" = ____"

7. **1/2 of (Dimension 2** ____" – dimension 5 ____")** = ____"

8. **Dimension 7** ____" + armhole depth ____" = ____"

9. **Dimension 8** ____" × 2 = ____"

Plan your front opening and neck finish (see pages 31–69).

A vest in stitches and rows

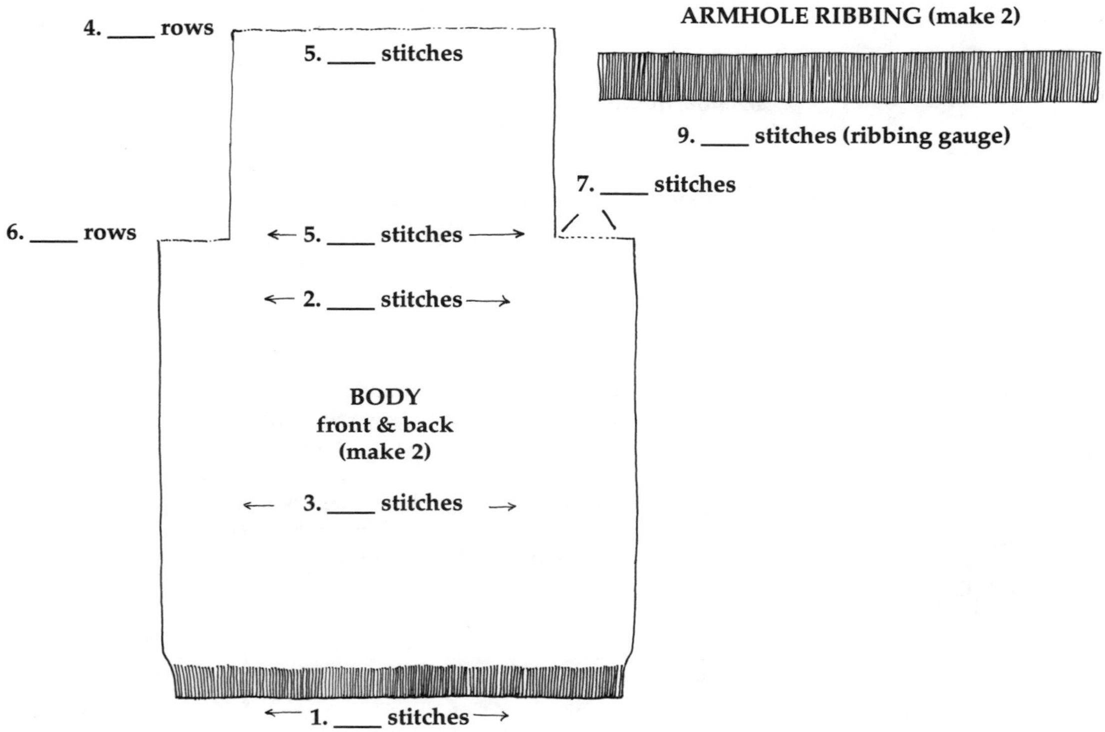

4. ____ rows

5. ____ stitches

ARMHOLE RIBBING (make 2)

9. ____ stitches (ribbing gauge)

7. ____ stitches

6. ____ rows

← **5. ____ stitches** →

← **2. ____ stitches** →

BODY
front & back
(make 2)

← **3. ____ stitches** →

← **1. ____ stitches** →

Multiply the dimensions in inches on page 102 by the gauge from your swatch; fill in all the blanks. Use stitches for the horizontal dimensions (—) and rows for the vertical dimensions (|).

Remember to figure out your neckline and front finish requirements. If your vest will have patterns, use the stitch and row counts to locate them on this chart.

Gauge
____ stitches/inch
____ rows/inch

Ribbing gauge
when stretched out
____ stitches/inch

Putting together a vest

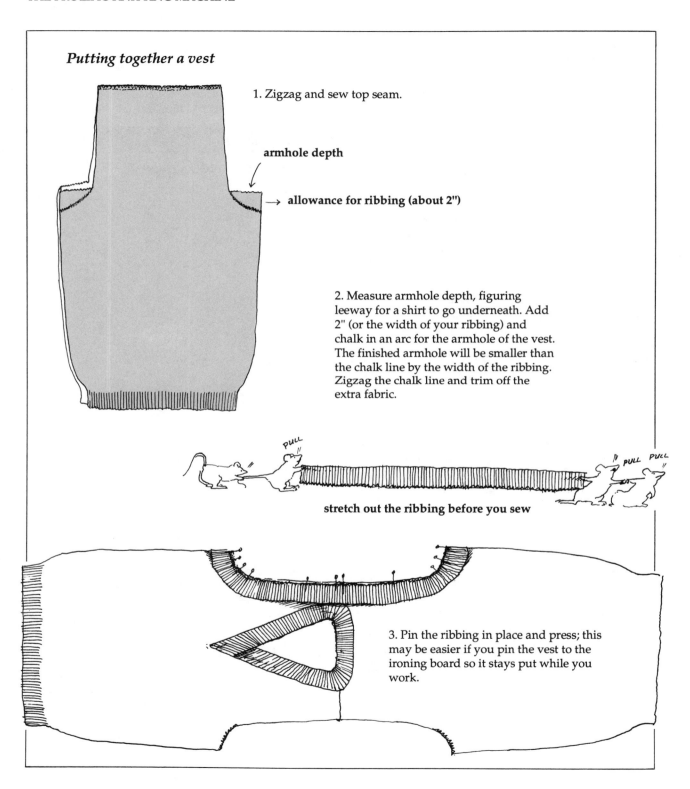

1. Zigzag and sew top seam.

armhole depth

→ **allowance for ribbing (about 2")**

2. Measure armhole depth, figuring leeway for a shirt to go underneath. Add 2" (or the width of your ribbing) and chalk in an arc for the armhole of the vest. The finished armhole will be smaller than the chalk line by the width of the ribbing. Zigzag the chalk line and trim off the extra fabric.

stretch out the ribbing before you sew

3. Pin the ribbing in place and press; this may be easier if you pin the vest to the ironing board so it stays put while you work.

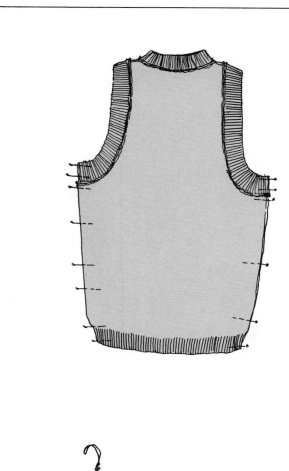

4. Press and pin the sides. Sew the seam close to the edge.

5. Press the armhole ribbing over the end of the ironing board until it's a flat oval.

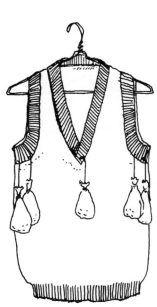

If the ribbing puckers the knitting, mist it with water and hang weights on it until it dries.

Capes

for the dramatic,
mysterious,
pregnant,
and growing

Capes

What could be better suited to a knitting machine than a cape? A knitting machine can purr out great lengths of fine, tight, unsagging knit in fabulous patterns and textures that would drive a hand knitter to early decrepitude. Do you have some swatches of really grandiose texture? Do you have some hugely complex patterns you want to show off? Make a cape!

Measure. (1) How long do you want your cape? (2) How wide should it be? Measure your "wingspan," from one wrist across your shoulders to the other wrist. That's all there is to measuring.

Design, calculate, and draft. Design your cape. There will be three pieces to knit for the body, and two seams to put them together. Incorporate those seams into your design or ignore them. Plan your collar or neck finish. Calculate the dimensions of the three pieces: the width of each is one-third of the wrist-to-wrist measurement, and its length is twice your favorite length (because the pieces run vertically, from front to back). Using your gauge, convert the measurements into stitches and rows on your draft.

Knit. Pin your design on the wall by your draft, for inspiration and information, and start knitting. There'll be no need to bother with ribbing or binding off. Remember, though, that you will be knitting bottom-to-top as you work the front, and top-to-bottom down the back.

Knit the entire garment. It takes a lot of yarn, doesn't it? Full the pieces and give them a good pressing.

Sew. Sew your collar or neck finish in place. Sew up the two body seams and press everything.

Put the cape on a cooperative person, a dressmaker's dummy, or a sturdy hanger. Chalk a hemline that's parallel to the floor. Spread the cape on the floor and even up the chalk line, then connect it all the way around. Zigzag along the line and trim away the excess fabric.

Measure the circumference of the cape—all the way around. Knit an edge binding a little longer than that; to get the number of rows multiply inches by row gauge. The edge binding should be 1½" to 2" wide, and you'll fold it in half. Sew your edge binding in place, as shown on page 00. Try to avoid either stretching or easing the knitting and the binding. Press everything.

Put on your new cape, and go look romantic or dashing. Stride and billow a bit, or wrap up and look mysterious.

Measurements for a cape

	Body	Adjustment (for ease, cutting, and seams)	Adjusted measurement
"Wingspan" (wrist to wrist across back)	____ "		
Cape length	____ "		

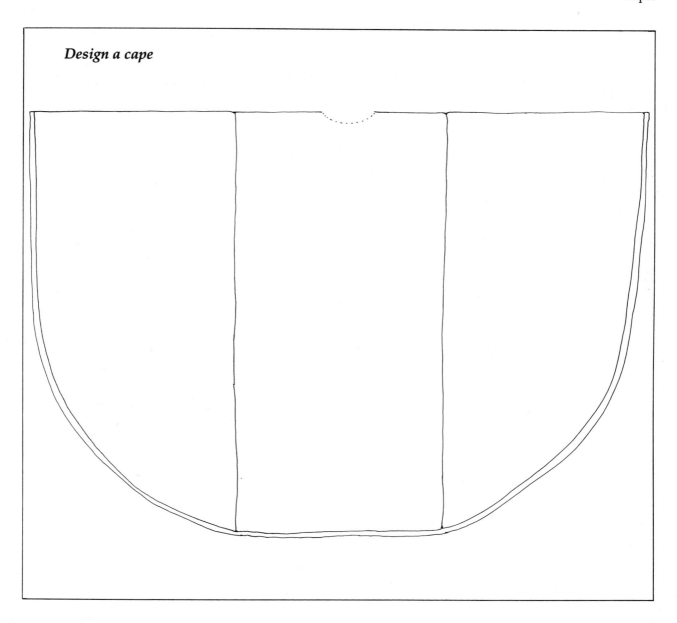

Design a cape

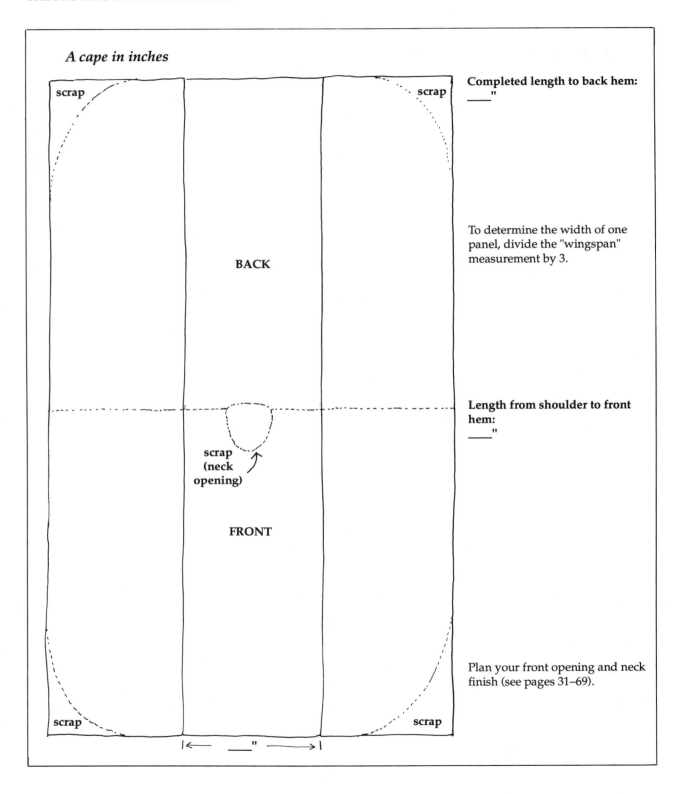

A cape in inches

scrap

scrap

BACK

Completed length to back hem:
___"

To determine the width of one panel, divide the "wingspan" measurement by 3.

scrap
(neck
opening)

FRONT

Length from shoulder to front hem:
___"

scrap

scrap

Plan your front opening and neck finish (see pages 31–69).

|← ___" →|

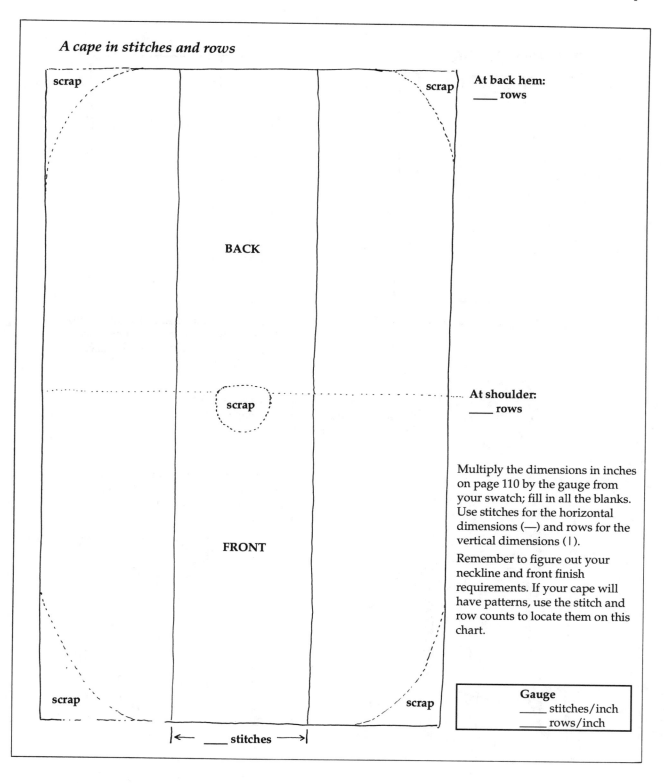

A cape in stitches and rows

scrap

scrap

At back hem:
____ rows

BACK

scrap

At shoulder:
____ rows

FRONT

scrap

scrap

|←— ____ stitches —→|

Multiply the dimensions in inches on page 110 by the gauge from your swatch; fill in all the blanks. Use stitches for the horizontal dimensions (—) and rows for the vertical dimensions (|).

Remember to figure out your neckline and front finish requirements. If your cape will have patterns, use the stitch and row counts to locate them on this chart.

Gauge
____ stitches/inch
____ rows/inch

Putting a cape together

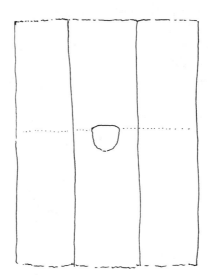

1. Press the knitting; sew the pieces together.

2. Find the shoulderline (halfway point). Center and put in your neckline finish; remember to place the shallow curve at the back neck.

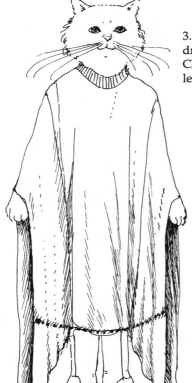

3. Put the cape on a cooperative person, a dressmaker's dummy, or a big hanger. Chalk a line about level with the desired length.

4. Lay the cape out flat and rechalk that line so it is a smooth, curved hemline. Zigzag along the line and trim away the extra fabric.

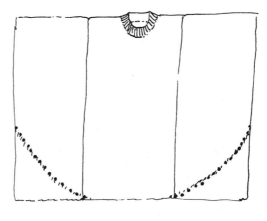

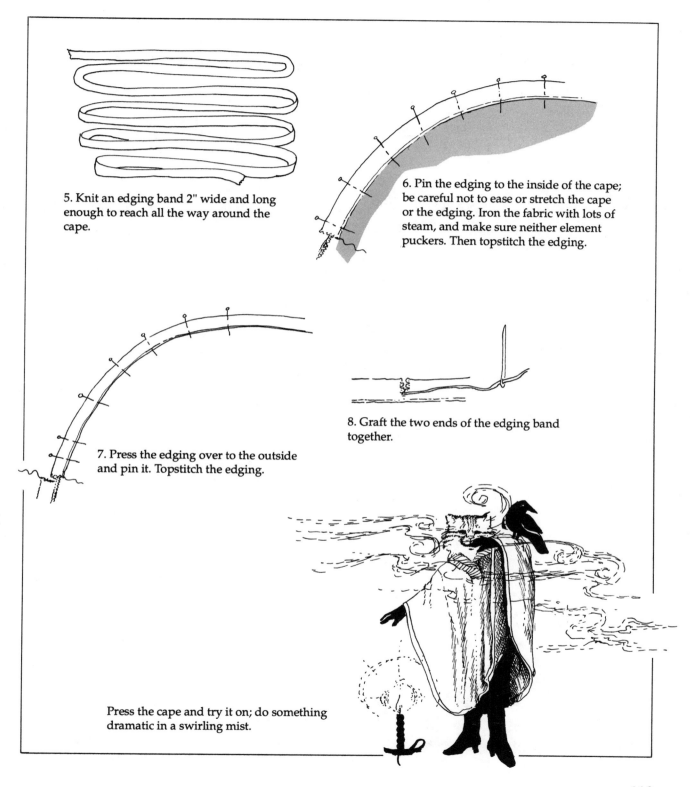

5. Knit an edging band 2" wide and long enough to reach all the way around the cape.

6. Pin the edging to the inside of the cape; be careful not to ease or stretch the cape or the edging. Iron the fabric with lots of steam, and make sure neither element puckers. Then topstitch the edging.

7. Press the edging over to the outside and pin it. Topstitch the edging.

8. Graft the two ends of the edging band together.

Press the cape and try it on; do something dramatic in a swirling mist.

Coats

Coats

Finding a great winter coat is a necessary, expensive, dreary experience for snow-belt people. Most winter coats are either the stiff, tailored sort (that feel as though you're wearing aluminum siding) or the down sort (that make you look like an inflatable toy). A sweater coat is warm and flexible, but the handknit ones get saggy and rump-sprung. If you've got a knitting machine, you can knit a firm fabric and create a perfect winter coat.

Design. Look for a swatch that is thick, firm, and dense. Fair Isle patterning will double the warmth in a coat. The knit fabric should not be loose, or the coat will sag as it reaches calf-length. The yarn should be sturdy and hard-wearing, because your coat may go a lot of places, and in some foul weather, too.

Measure. Take the same measurements as for a sweater: chest, hip, arm, wrist, and length as far down as you want your coat. Measure from the outer edge of one shoulder to the outer edge of the other.

Place a tape measure or yardstick on the floor, stride your legs apart as if walking briskly, and measure how big around you need the coat to be at the hem for those times when you have to chase the dog or climb gracefully into a truck. Sixty inches is right for me. Plan to make side panels for your coat, because your knitting bed probably can't handle the width in two pieces. Even if it could, the coat would be saggy, pointy, and weird along its side seams.

Add 8" to 10" to the hip and chest measurements, because a coat may need to fit over a lot of other clothing. Add 4" or 5" to the wrist measurement for the same reason.

Measurements for a coat
(See pages 16–19 for how to measure.)

	Body	Adjustment (for ease, cutting, and seams)	Adjusted measurement
Chest	___ "	+ 8–10" ease	___ "
Hips	___ "	+ 8–10" ease	___ "
Shoulders	___ "		
Armhole depth	___ "	+ 3"	___ "
Wrist	___ "	+ 4–5" ease	___ "
Arm length	___ "		
Coat length *(shoulder to hem)*	___ "		
Stride *(see text above)*	___ "		

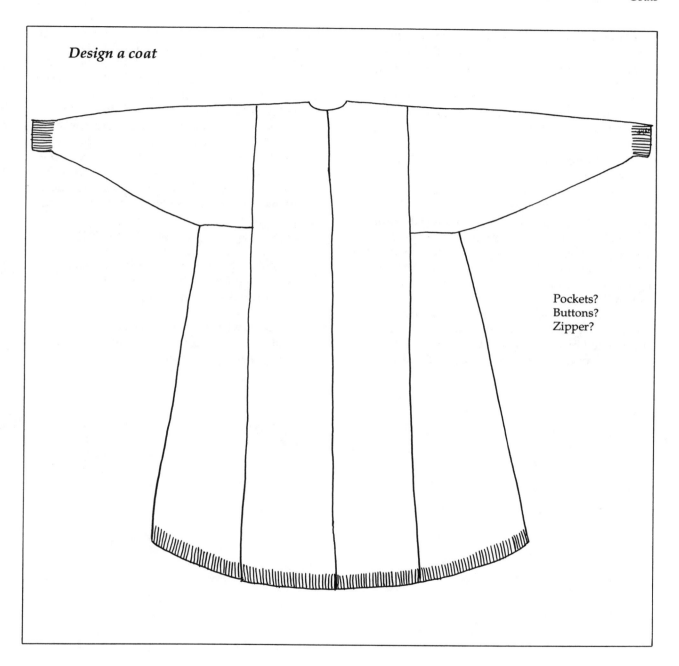

Design a coat

Pockets?
Buttons?
Zipper?

Plan. The front and back panels are as wide as your shoulder-width measurement. They are as long as your desired coat length, plus 1" for cutting and seaming.

The sleeve length is your arm measurement (to the nape of the neck) minus half the panel width. The cuff ribbing is your wrist measurement plus 4" or 5".

Measure from the shoulder down to 3" past the armpit seam on your shirt sleeve. That will give you the armhole depth; double the number to get the width at the top of the sleeve. You will have to complete the increases to reach that width before your side panel meets your sleeve, though, because you knit straight where the sleeve and side panel join—we'll handle that bit in a minute. First we'll figure out how to shape the side panels: bottom, top, and length.

The bottoms of the side panels make up the difference between the total hem width and what is contributed by the front and back panels. For instance, if your hem is to be 60" around and your shoulders measure 15", the front and back panels will measure 15" each, for a total of 30". The side panels will need to add a total of 30" at their bottoms—which works out to 15" on each side, or per panel—to produce the 60".

The tops of the side panels provide the difference between the circumference of your chest plus 8" or so of ease and what is contributed by the front and back panels. For instance, say your chest-plus-8" is 48". Your shoulders are 15", so the front and back panels give 30" (again). Then the side panels will need to add a total of 18" at their tops, or 9" per panel, to reach the full 48".

The length of each side panel is the length of the coat minus the armhole depth.

Remember the top width of the side panel? For our example, it is 9". Take half that width, in this case, 4½". You'll stop increasing on the sleeve 4½" from the top.

Figure out what sort of front opening you want your coat to have, and reread the appropriate sections on pages 31–57.

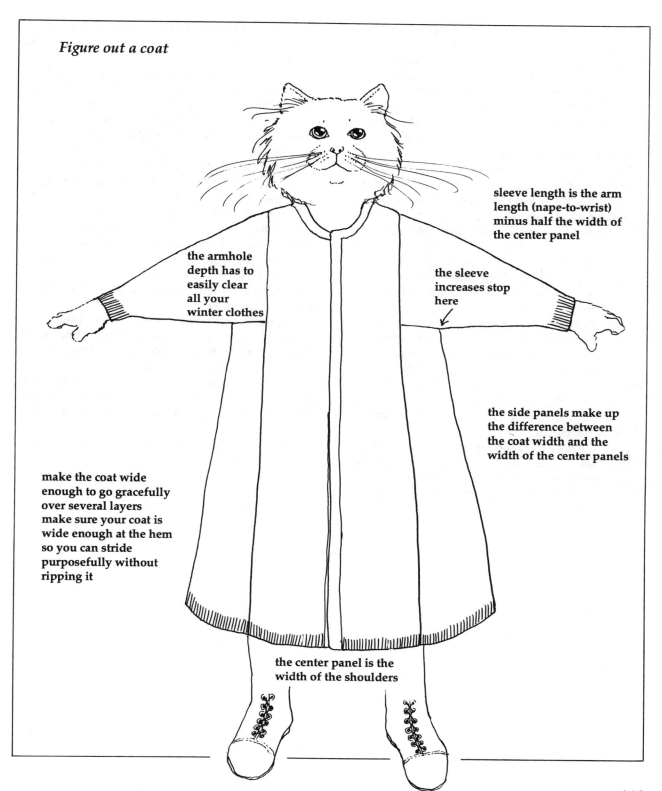

Figure out a coat

sleeve length is the arm length (nape-to-wrist) minus half the width of the center panel

the armhole depth has to easily clear all your winter clothes

the sleeve increases stop here

the side panels make up the difference between the coat width and the width of the center panels

make the coat wide enough to go gracefully over several layers make sure your coat is wide enough at the hem so you can stride purposefully without ripping it

the center panel is the width of the shoulders

Draft and calculate. Knit a large gauge swatch and full it. Figure your gauge and multiply through your calculations to make a knitting draft.

Estimate a decrease rate for the side panels. Subtract the number of stitches at the top from the number of stitches at the bottom. Divide the result into the number of rows in the length. Multiply the answer by two, because you decrease one stitch on each side, every that-many rows.

Estimate an increase rate for the sleeves. Subtract the number of cuff stitches from the number of stitches at the top of the sleeve. Measure the increasing part of each sleeve, or subtract half of the top width of a side panel from the total length of the sleeve above the cuff. Divide the difference between cuff and top into the number of rows in the increasing part. Multiply the answer by two, because again you increase one stitch at each side every that-many rows.

Knit. Rib the bottom hem of your coat more loosely than usual, so it will not pucker around your calves. Knit the pieces according to your draft. I usually knit the side panels a little longer than I've drafted, so I can unravel them to the exact row as I sew the parts together.

Full the pieces and repair any dropped stitches. Press all the pieces.

Sew. Zigzag across the tops of the front and back panels. Pin the top edges together and press them smooth, then sew them together directly under the zigzag stitching. Open up the seam and press it smooth.

Chalk in the neck opening and front opening, and finish according to your choice of the possibilities on pages 31–57.

Zigzag across the tops of the sleeves, stretching them out a little as you sew. Press them. Working one at a time, center each sleeve on one of the shoulder seams of the panels. Pin the sleeves in place, stretching them out a little, and press the body and sleeve together so they won't curl so much. Sew the sleeves to the body, keeping the seams as close to the edges as possible. Open up and press each seam.

Pin one side panel in place. Press the body and the side together, so they won't curl. Sew them together to the last 1/4" before the sleeve, then sew the other side of the side panel in place. Sew the other panel in the same way.

Unravel each side panel back to the sleeve line. Zigzag across the top.

Pin, press, and sew the sleeve seams along the increased part. Pin the top of each side panel across the open end of the associated sleeve. Press as well as you can; this is a dodgy little area. Sew across, leaving 1/4" open at each corner. It's very difficult to get the corners perfect, and I always prefer to fidget them into place with a steam iron and needle and thread.

Turn everything right side out, and give it all a good pressing.

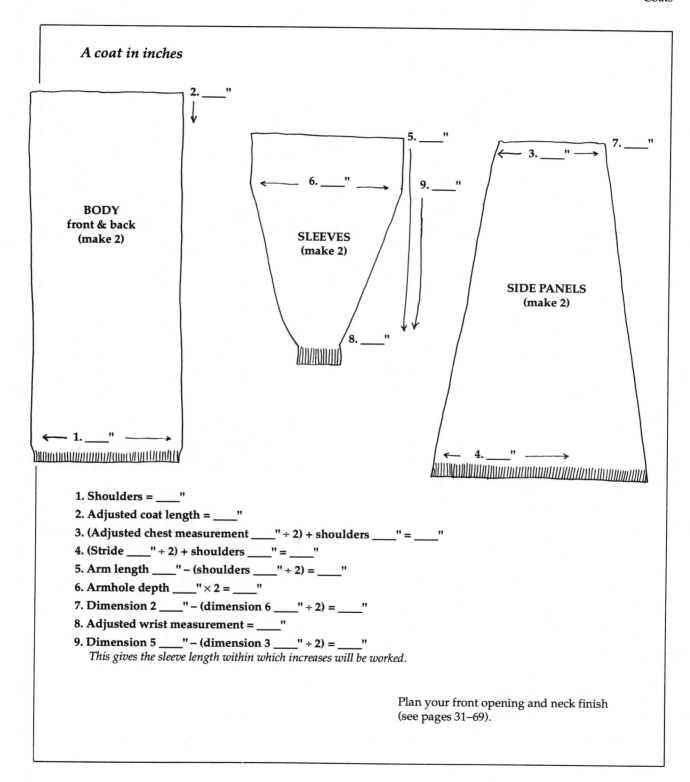

A coat in inches

2. ____"

**BODY
front & back
(make 2)**

5. ____"

6. ____"

9. ____"

**SLEEVES
(make 2)**

8. ____"

3. ____"

7. ____"

**SIDE PANELS
(make 2)**

1. ____"

4. ____"

1. **Shoulders = ____"**

2. **Adjusted coat length = ____"**

3. **(Adjusted chest measurement ____" ÷ 2) + shoulders ____" = ____"**

4. **(Stride ____" ÷ 2) + shoulders ____" = ____"**

5. **Arm length ____" – (shoulders ____" ÷ 2) = ____"**

6. **Armhole depth ____" × 2 = ____"**

7. **Dimension 2 ____" – (dimension 6 ____" ÷ 2) = ____"**

8. **Adjusted wrist measurement = ____"**

9. **Dimension 5 ____" – (dimension 3 ____" ÷ 2) = ____"**
   This gives the sleeve length within which increases will be worked.

Plan your front opening and neck finish
(see pages 31–69).

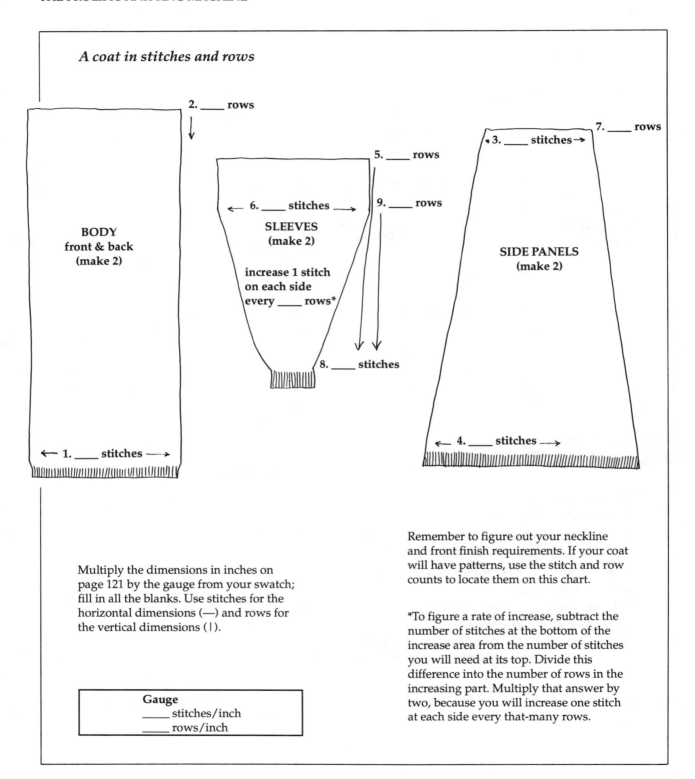

A coat in stitches and rows

2. ____ rows

7. ____ rows

5. ____ rows

◄ 3. ____ stitches ►

← 6. ____ stitches →

9. ____ rows

BODY
front & back
(make 2)

SLEEVES
(make 2)

increase 1 stitch
on each side
every ____ rows*

SIDE PANELS
(make 2)

8. ____ stitches

← 1. ____ stitches → →

← 4. ____ stitches →

Multiply the dimensions in inches on page 121 by the gauge from your swatch; fill in all the blanks. Use stitches for the horizontal dimensions (—) and rows for the vertical dimensions (|).

Remember to figure out your neckline and front finish requirements. If your coat will have patterns, use the stitch and row counts to locate them on this chart.

*To figure a rate of increase, subtract the number of stitches at the bottom of the increase area from the number of stitches you will need at its top. Divide this difference into the number of rows in the increasing part. Multiply that answer by two, because you will increase one stitch at each side every that-many rows.

Gauge
____ stitches/inch
____ rows/inch

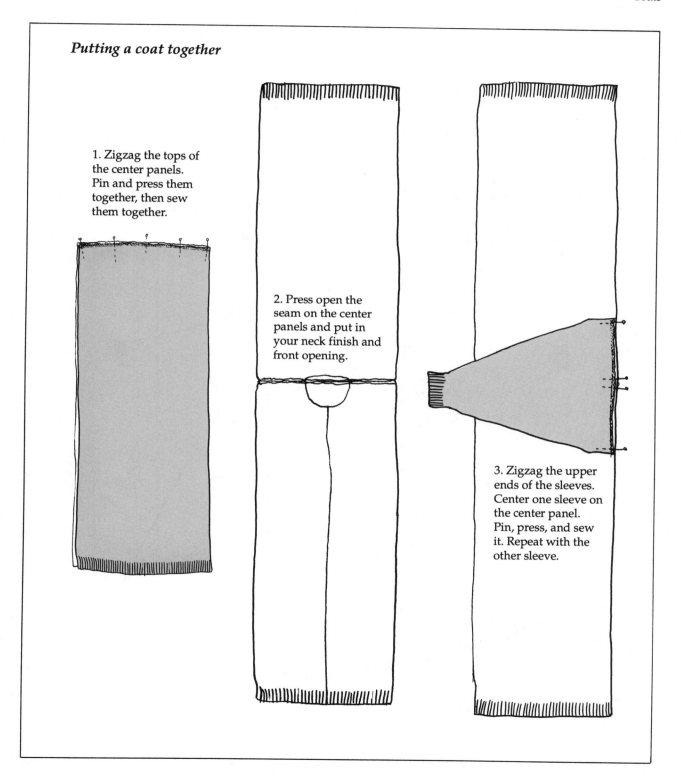

Putting a coat together

1. Zigzag the tops of the center panels. Pin and press them together, then sew them together.

2. Press open the seam on the center panels and put in your neck finish and front opening.

3. Zigzag the upper ends of the sleeves. Center one sleeve on the center panel. Pin, press, and sew it. Repeat with the other sleeve.

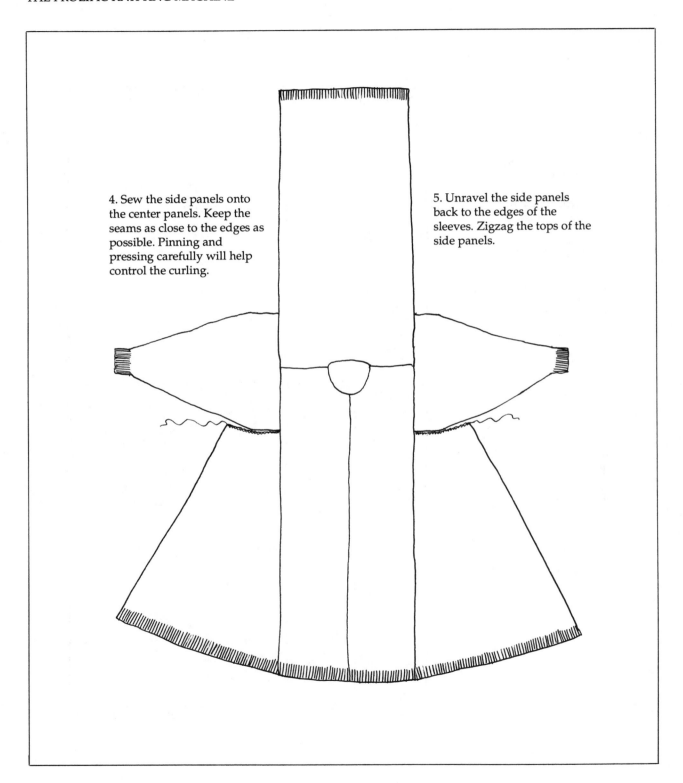

4. Sew the side panels onto the center panels. Keep the seams as close to the edges as possible. Pinning and pressing carefully will help control the curling.

5. Unravel the side panels back to the edges of the sleeves. Zigzag the tops of the side panels.

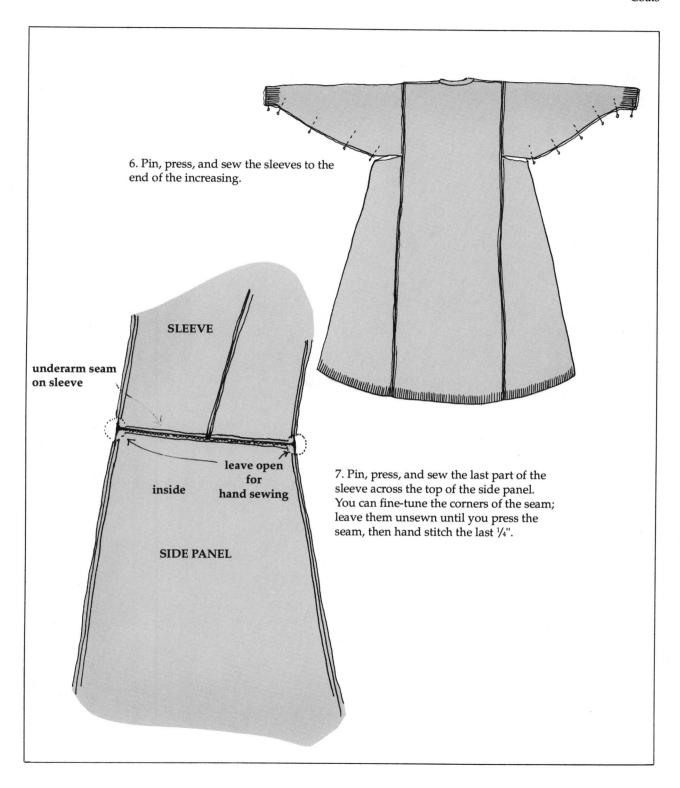

6. Pin, press, and sew the sleeves to the end of the increasing.

SLEEVE

underarm seam on sleeve

leave open for hand sewing

inside

SIDE PANEL

7. Pin, press, and sew the last part of the sleeve across the top of the side panel. You can fine-tune the corners of the seam; leave them unsewn until you press the seam, then hand stitch the last 1/4".

Big
People

Big people

If your widest part is over 50" around, your knitting machine may not embrace you with only a front and a back. Even if you could make very wide knitting, the proportions of body to sleeves could look better. Side panels solve both problems.

Measure. Take the usual measurements for a sweater. If necklines are usually uncomfortable, make that measurement loose. Measure wrist and upper arm, and look for a comfortable armhole depth. A shoulder-to-shoulder measurement provides a good width for front and back panels. If your sweater is to be thigh-length, the circumference of the hem of the sweater will need to measure at least as much as the circumference of your

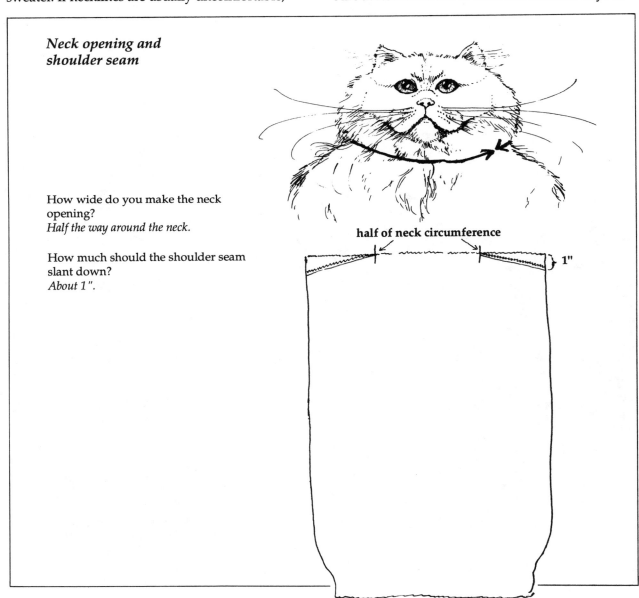

Neck opening and shoulder seam

How wide do you make the neck opening?
Half the way around the neck.

How much should the shoulder seam slant down?
About 1".

half of neck circumference

1"

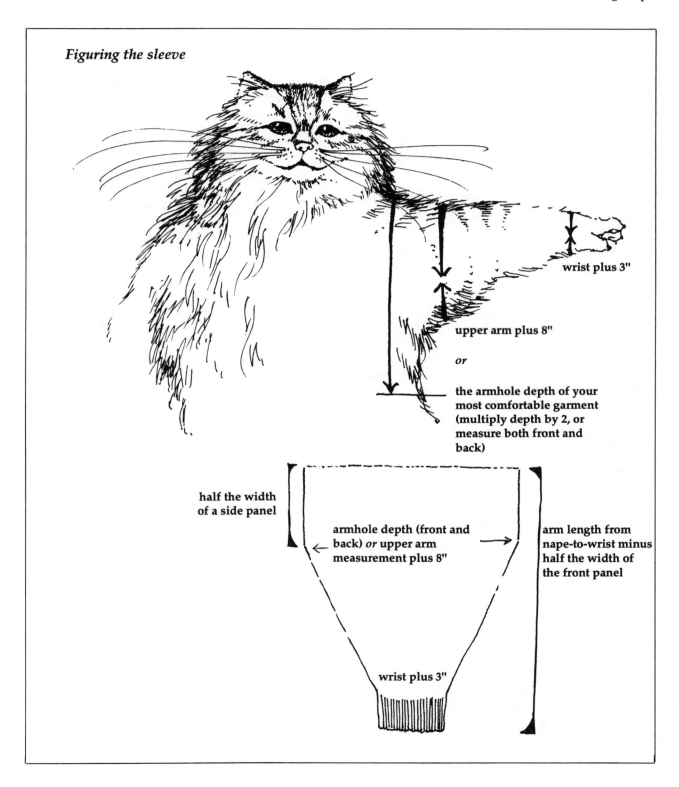

Figuring the sleeve

wrist plus 3"

upper arm plus 8"

or

the armhole depth of your
most comfortable garment
(multiply depth by 2, or
measure both front and
back)

half the width
of a side panel

armhole depth (front and
back) *or* upper arm
measurement plus 8"

arm length from
nape-to-wrist minus
half the width of
the front panel

wrist plus 3"

widest part.

Calculate and draft. Calculate the front and back panels first. Make them as wide as the shoulder-to-shoulder measurement and as long as you like.

Calculate the sleeves next. Subtract half the front panel width from the nape-to-wrist arm length: that's how long the sleeves will be. Add 3" to the wrist measurement to get your cast-on width. Add at least 8" to the upper arm measurement. See if double your armhole depth is about that much. I like comfortable sleeves, so I make the top of the sleeve the wider of these two measurements.

Now figure the side panels. Add as much ease as you want to your horizontal measurements to get a total garment width. Subtract from this the width of the front and back panels, and divide the leftover amount into two side panels. If your hips are much wider than your chest, you can make sides which are wider at the bottom than at the top, exactly as they are figured for the coat (page 118). If your chest and hips are nearly the same, the panels can be straight up-and-down. The measurements will tell you how many cast-on stitches and how many stitches across the top you will need. To get the length of the side panels, subtract the armhole depth from the length of the center panels.

When you know how wide your side panels will be at the top, you can finish figuring the sleeves. Divide that number in half. You'll stop increasing the sleeve when it meets the side panel, so subtract the number you just got from the sleeve length. By the time your sleeve reaches this new length, you'll need to have completed the increases.

Plan your collar or neck finish.

That should do you for calculations; multiply all the inches by your stitch and row gauges to get your knitting draft.

Knit. Make all the pieces according to your draft. Full them, then fix any glitches. Measure the pieces to see if they are the sizes you want, and adjust them if they are not.

Sew. Join the front and back center panels. The shoulders will need a little slope, 1" down for every 3" across. Make the neck opening about half as wide as the neck's circumference. Put on the neck finish or collar.

Zigzag the tops of the sleeves. Center the tops of the sleeves on the shoulder seams, and stretch them out gently as you press and pin them into position. Sew them in place.

Stop and make sure your side panels are long enough to meet the sleeves. If they're short, rehang them and knit a little extra. I always knit them extra long in the first place, and do some cutting or unraveling until they fit.

Sew the side panels to the bottoms of the front and back. Sew the sleeve seams up to the point

Measurements for big people
(See pages 16–19 for how to measure.)

	Body	Adjustment (for ease, cutting, and seams)	Adjusted measurement
Neck	____"		
Chest	____"	+ 6–8" ease + 1" seam allowance	____"
Waist	____"	+ 6–8" ease + 1" seam allowance	____"
Hips	____"	+ 6–8" ease + 1" seam allowance	____"
Shoulders	____"		
Upper arm	____"	+ 8"	____"
Armhole depth	____"		
Wrist	____"	+ 4"	____"
Arm length	____"		
Sweater length	____"	+ 8"	____"

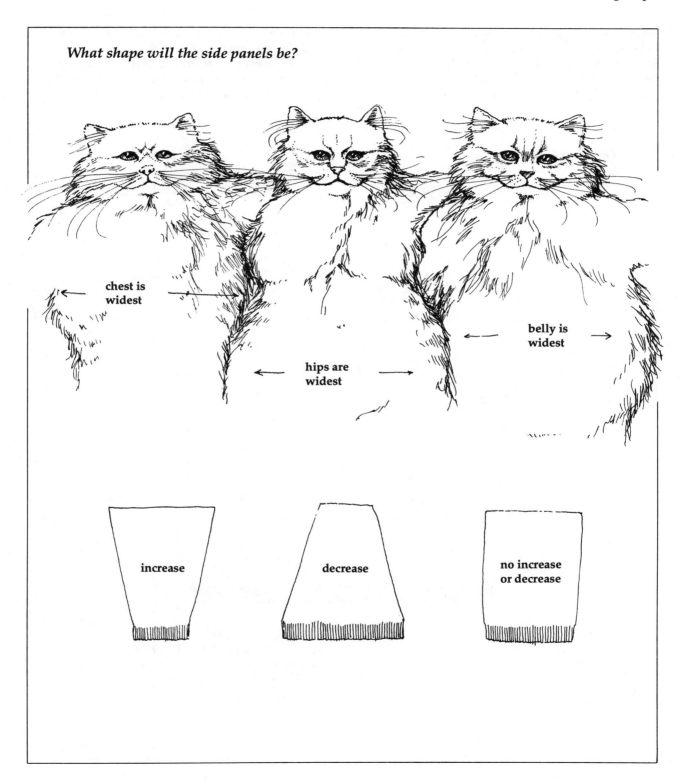

What shape will the side panels be?

chest is widest

hips are widest

belly is widest

increase

decrease

no increase or decrease

where you stopped decreasing. Pin the tops of the side panels to the remaining sections of the sleeves, and sew them up. I don't sew into the corners of those seams too far, leaving the last ¼" to be hand stitched after the seams have been pressed. Knit-ting and wild beasts are both dangerous when chased into corners.

Go over everything thoroughly with the steam iron. Tidy up any dropped stitches. Press again. Put the sweater on, and admire yourself!

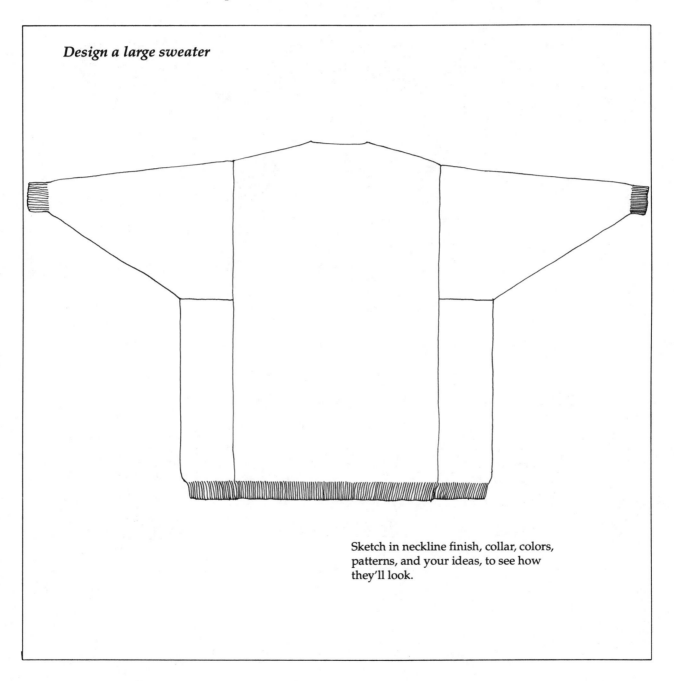

Design a large sweater

Sketch in neckline finish, collar, colors, patterns, and your ideas, to see how they'll look.

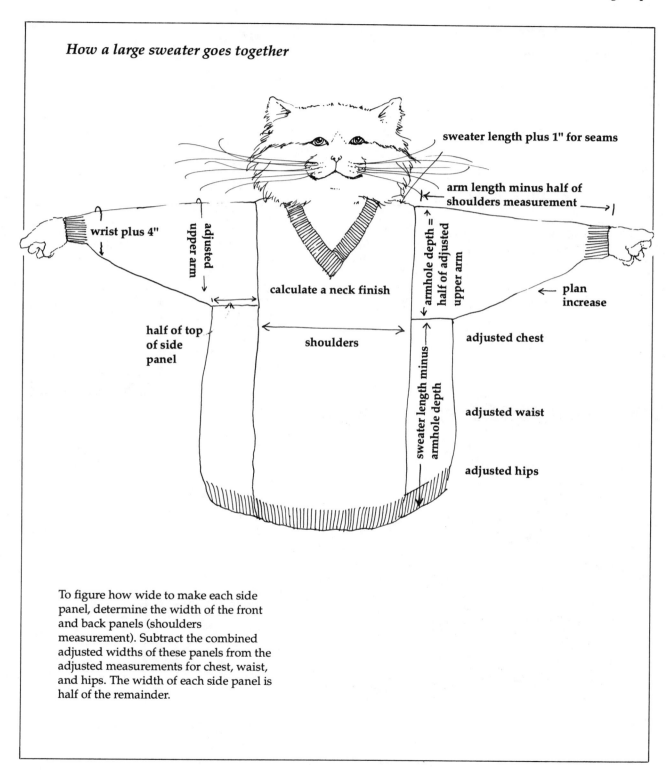

How a large sweater goes together

sweater length plus 1" for seams

arm length minus half of shoulders measurement

wrist plus 4"

adjusted upper arm

armhole depth = half of adjusted upper arm

calculate a neck finish

plan increase

half of top of side panel

shoulders

adjusted chest

sweater length minus armhole depth

adjusted waist

adjusted hips

To figure how wide to make each side panel, determine the width of the front and back panels (shoulders measurement). Subtract the combined adjusted widths of these panels from the adjusted measurements for chest, waist, and hips. The width of each side panel is half of the remainder.

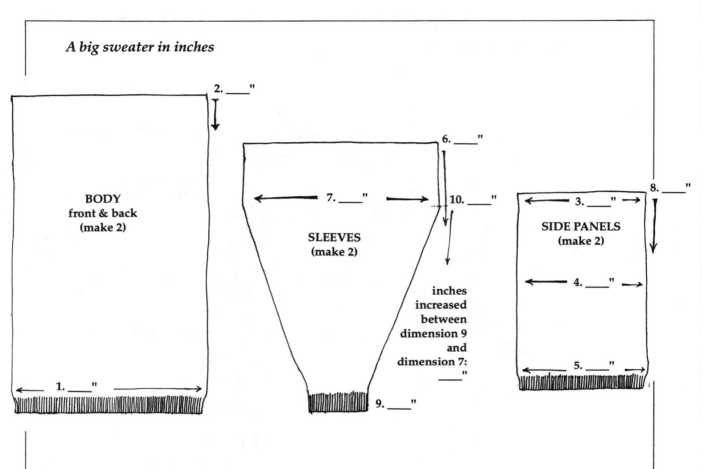

A big sweater in inches

2. ____"

BODY
front & back
(make 2)

1. ____"

6. ____"

7. ____"

10. ____"

SLEEVES
(make 2)

inches
increased
between
dimension 9
and
dimension 7:
____"

9. ____"

3. ____"

8. ____"

SIDE PANELS
(make 2)

4. ____"

5. ____"

1. **Shoulders = ____"**

2. **Adjusted sweater length = ____"**

3. **(Adjusted chest measurement ____" ÷ 2) – dimension 1 ____" = ____"**

4. **(Adjusted waist measurement ____" ÷ 2) – dimension 1 ____" = ____"**

5. **(Adjusted hip measurement ____" ÷ 2) – dimension 1 ____" = ____"**

6. **Arm length ____" – (1/2 of dimension 1 ____") = ____"**

7. *For the width of the sleeve, choose the larger of the following measurements:*
   Armhole depth ____" × 2 = ____"
   Adjusted upper arm measurement = ____"

8. **Dimension 2 ____" – (1/2 of dimension 7 ____") = ____"**

9. **Adjusted wrist measurement = ____"**

10. **Dimension 6 ____" – (1/2 of dimension 3 ____") = ____"**
    This gives the length of sleeve over which the decreases will be worked.

Plan your front opening and neck finish
(see pages 31–69).

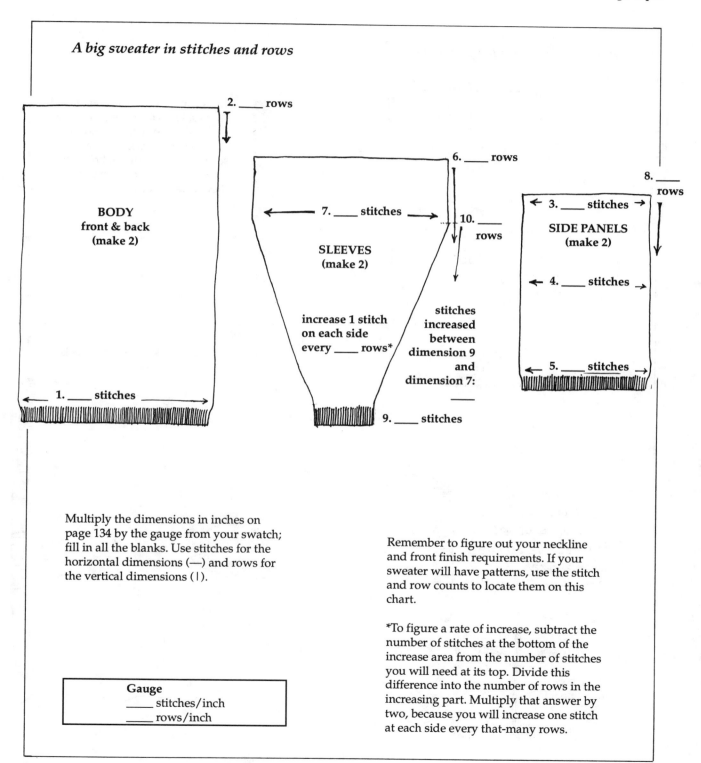

A big sweater in stitches and rows

2. ____ rows

6. ____ rows

8. ____ rows

BODY
front & back
(make 2)

SLEEVES
(make 2)

7. ____ stitches

10. ____ rows

3. ____ stitches

SIDE PANELS
(make 2)

4. ____ stitches

increase 1 stitch
on each side
every ____ rows*

stitches
increased
between
dimension 9
and
dimension 7:

____

5. ____ stitches

1. ____ stitches

9. ____ stitches

Multiply the dimensions in inches on page 134 by the gauge from your swatch; fill in all the blanks. Use stitches for the horizontal dimensions (—) and rows for the vertical dimensions (│).

Gauge
____ stitches/inch
____ rows/inch

Remember to figure out your neckline and front finish requirements. If your sweater will have patterns, use the stitch and row counts to locate them on this chart.

*To figure a rate of increase, subtract the number of stitches at the bottom of the increase area from the number of stitches you will need at its top. Divide this difference into the number of rows in the increasing part. Multiply that answer by two, because you will increase one stitch at each side every that-many rows.

Putting together a large sweater

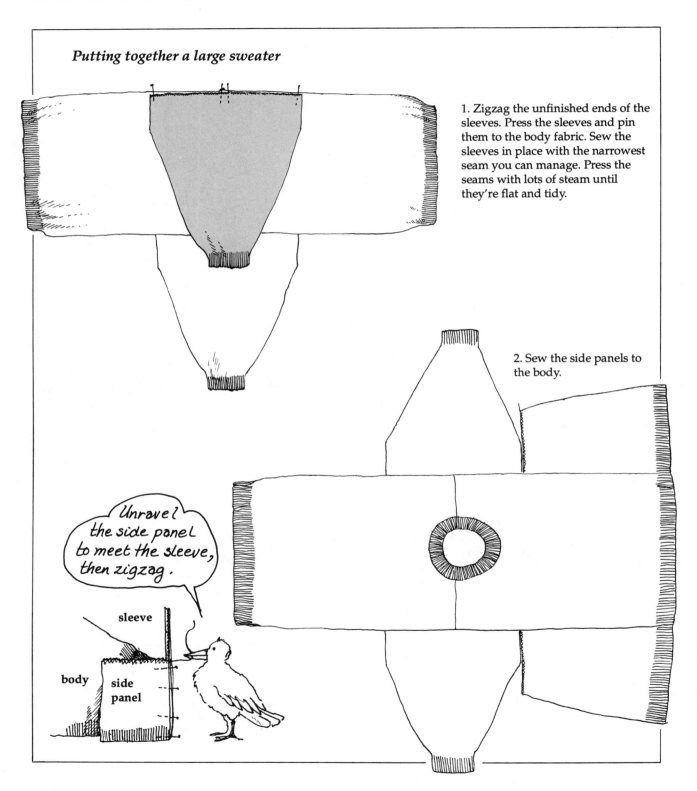

1. Zigzag the unfinished ends of the sleeves. Press the sleeves and pin them to the body fabric. Sew the sleeves in place with the narrowest seam you can manage. Press the seams with lots of steam until they're flat and tidy.

2. Sew the side panels to the body.

Unravel the side panel to meet the sleeve, then zigzag.

sleeve

body

side panel

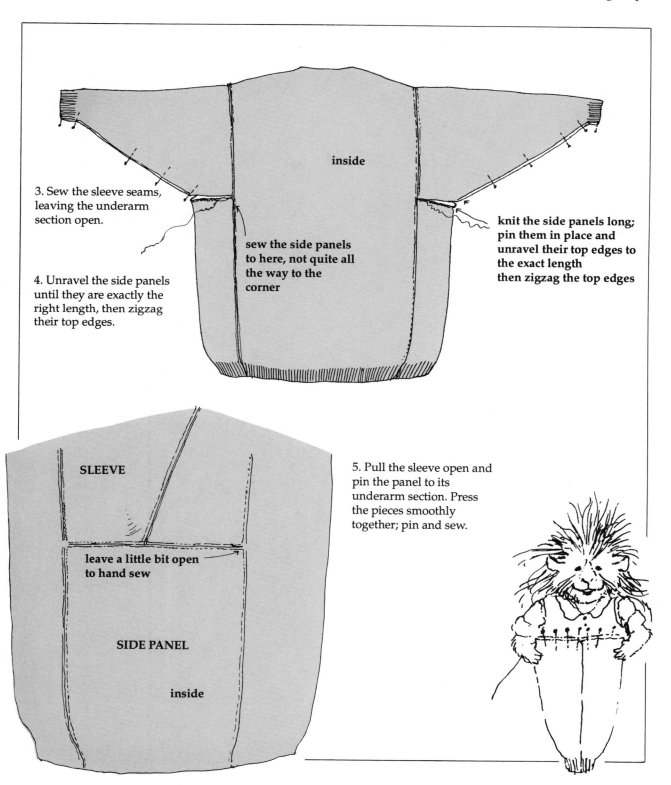

3. Sew the sleeve seams, leaving the underarm section open.

4. Unravel the side panels until they are exactly the right length, then zigzag their top edges.

inside

sew the side panels to here, not quite all the way to the corner

knit the side panels long; pin them in place and unravel their top edges to the exact length then zigzag the top edges

SLEEVE

leave a little bit open to hand sew

SIDE PANEL

inside

5. Pull the sleeve open and pin the panel to its underarm section. Press the pieces smoothly together; pin and sew.

137

Little
People

Little people

When you were a child, you had favorite colors, and favorite things, and knew exactly what clothes you wanted to wear. No one understood what wonderful ideas you had for clothes, or what subtle color combinations you had dreamed up, unless you found a rare adult who not only asked what you wanted but also listened. When you make a sweater for a child, *ask* and *listen!* Children, as soon as they can talk at all, will tell you exactly what they want, and they have perfect, individual taste and style.

Making a child's sweater, then, is no different than making an adult's sweater. Take the same measurements. Ask the same questions about color, pattern, length, and style. Offer your box of test swatches to choose from. There are only a few extra considerations.

Children grow. They grow more up than out, and their limbs grow fastest. Add between 2" and 3" to the sleeve length, and make the ribbing between 4" and 6" long. Roll the sleeve up twice the first year, once the second year, and not at all the third year. Add 8" to the chest and hip measurement. Children may not thicken much, but they need room for rowdiness. Add 2" to the length that fits now.

Children get dirty. They play especially hard in garments they love. The yarn needs to be launderable. Save fluffy, delicate yarn for demure and refined stages. Save pastel colors, too, for sudden surges of fastidiousness.

Children may have difficulty with buttons and an awful time with separating zippers. Do not send a child to school in a garment that the teacher will have to fasten before recess. Consult Mom about fastenings; Velcro® may be the answer.

Children lose things. A hood will not be lost, while a cap might. Should you attach mittens to a sweater with crocheted cord? Would it help to knit a name or initials in?

Very, very young children need a few more considerations.

Babies' heads are large in proportion to their bodies. A collar will have to open up wide, then close up far enough not to slide off their shoulders. Zippers are better than buttons, because a really industrious chewer can nip off a button.

Babies are damp, and decorate themselves with sticky, sweet smears. The yarn must endure frequent and vigorous laundering. The colors should not be inconvenienced by juice, jam, and indigestion.

Babies do not dress themselves, and may be impatient with those who perform this task for them. Someone bigger must reach into baby's sleeve to pull the pudgy little arm through, so make cuffs as wide around as a bigger person's fist. Baby may protest being squeezed through a crewneck. Baby may be enraged at being forced through a turtleneck. Use V-necks, shawl collars, and zips. Ask the baby's grown-up friends what's easiest to handle. Copy what works.

Babies crawl. A smooth, firm yarn that will not pill is needed for mileage. A fluffy yarn, bellied around the carpet and maneuvered into mischief, will soon look grim. Choose colors that don't show road wear.

Babies drool. Cut a V-neck below the water line and let a T-shirt do the sopping up.

Babies may also have tender skin or undiscovered allergies. When in doubt, use cotton yarn.

If the child for whom you are knitting is in the least able to communicate, schedule a direct consultation. Children know what they like and don't like. Ask questions and listen. The results will be splendid!

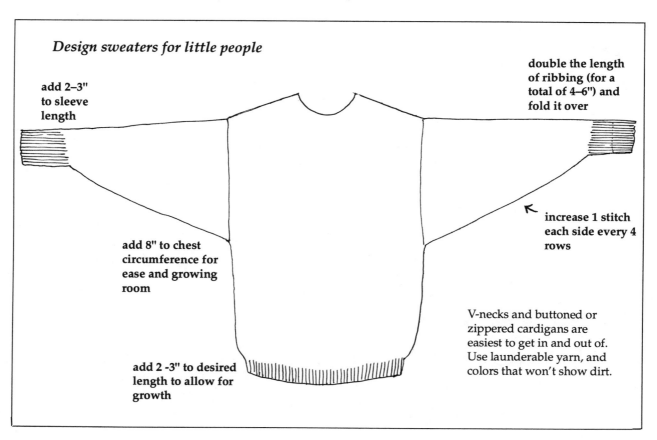

Design sweaters for little people

add 2–3" to sleeve length

double the length of ribbing (for a total of 4–6") and fold it over

add 8" to chest circumference for ease and growing room

increase 1 stitch each side every 4 rows

add 2 -3" to desired length to allow for growth

V-necks and buttoned or zippered cardigans are easiest to get in and out of. Use launderable yarn, and colors that won't show dirt.

Extraordinary People

Catherine Cartwright-Jones

Extraordinary people

Is your body of absolutely ordinary size, of ordinary weight, with every part in ordinary proportion, and all working in an absolutely ordinary way? If, next Tuesday after lunch, some part of you is abruptly out of working order, would you lose your fondness for beautiful, well-made, perfectly fitted clothes? Would you cheerfully become a fashion nonentity?

Zylvi, your friend, would love a sweater with one-and-one-half sleeves that fits nicely, so she can go skiing. She would like it in a mauvy color, with no unfilled appendage that has to be caught up with a diaper pin. Her short arm works, but not when encased in an elephant's trunk of flopping sleeve. She hasn't seen a sweater that meets her needs in a shopping mall yet.

When your mobility is very limited, a friend can most easily dress you from the front. You'll want a garment with an opening in the back, and with Velcro® spots to close it. Buttons and zippers in back are painful or hazardous.

This is the same band that you use for cardigans, but without buttons or buttonholes.

A vest, a lap rug, and two tickets on the 50-yard line! Whee!

A program over here and two hot dogs!

Robert, her lover, wants to go to the snow, too, but needs a sweater that opens up the back, so Zylvi can help him dress. Quadriplegics have shortened torsos, and Robert needs a sweater wide enough to fit over his back brace, and cuffs that will pull on over the braces that keep his hands straight and useful.

Heidi, another friend, has glorious ideas for knitting, but can't find anyone who will "listen" as she talks through her word board.

Knitting for Zylvi, Robert, Heidi, or anyone with an extraordinary body, requires excellent listening skills more than knitting skills. Every extraordinary body is one-of-a-kind. The owner of that body knows what is needed. The knitter must only ask questions, take measurements, and listen, listen, listen.

Try the questions on the following pages.

145

What do you need most? You know best what you need, but you might guess wrong about what someone else needs. Ask.

What about sweaters is inconvenient or impossible? And, ***What would make a sweater perfect for you?*** Draw necessary changes on your design.

Can you manage buttons? Would a zipper or Velcro® be easier? Plan a garment that does not hinder.

Do you need the sweater to close in back? Make an opening in the back as you would in the front of a cardigan. Bind the opening with an edging strip (page 00) and sew in spots of Velcro®. Sitting on buttons or zippers is painful or dangerous.

Would a lot of pockets be useful? Draw in pockets as needed on the design.

What colors make you feel happiest? Everyone looks best in the colors they enjoy most.

Are there some mechanical bits that would catch on loose knits? Some people have braces or bionic elements to wear, that might get tangled in long Fair Isle floats, loose knits, fuzzies, or laces. The insides of their garments may need to be smooth and firm. Some people have knobs and gadgets on their chairs that would catch on loose yarn, or rub fuzzballs out of fluff. The outsides of their garments may need to be smooth and firm. Rub your test swatches over the contraptions to see what gets caught.

Do you need a hood on the sweater, or a matching cap? If picking up a lost cap is impossible and body temperature is not well regulated, go for a hood.

Would a cape be more useful? A cape that goes over a wheelchair keeps weather out, and sometimes also fends off intruding questions, when you're not in the mood for them.

Which of these test swatches do you like best?

147

Do you need a sweater that can be laundered? Use cotton or acrylic if the unexpected is commonplace.

Where should I take extra measurements so you'll have a good fit?

Do you need some mittens, fingerless gloves, or gloves? Would it be helpful to have a cord from the mittens to the sleeves, so they can be retrieved if dropped? Should we sew suede scraps onto the palms of the gloves, so you can mush a wheelchair through the snow?

Extraordinary people may have exquisite taste, and many would be elegant dressers if they had not been chucked into a fashion cosmic black hole. You will never know how quickly people can assume you have oatmeal for brains until you have some obvious physical malfunction. Anyone who does not think you still have taste, style, and intelligence should be bulldozed by a stampede of wheelchairs and then reminded that Steven Hawking is still Lucasian Professor of Mathematics at Cambridge. Motor neuron disease did not make him forget his sums. *Of course* your extraordinary friend—or you in the same position—can choose a favorite swatch.

Design your extraordinary sweater the same way you design other sweaters. Draw the answers to the questions into your sweater design. Write all the measurements into the calculations sheet. Translate the measurements into a draft. Knit the sweater. Sew it up. Take the extraordinary sweater to the extraordinary person, and cruise a nice, fluffy snowstorm together.

Caps & Berets

Caps

Did you ever look at the way a flat paper map can be made to fit over a globe? Little wedges are cut and fitted to meet at the poles. On my third-grade classroom globe, the darts didn't quite line up over Norway, and Oslo was crooked. Handknit caps have decreasing rows that make darts to fit the roundness of a head. Knitting-machine patterns for caps also have decreasing rows, but fiddling them along by transferring small bunches of stitches, or knitting little peaks while the rest of the stitches are on hold, is tiresome.

Make your cap with globe-fitter's cuts—half-fashion it to shape! If you keep the patterns and stripes on the bottom half of the cap, you won't run into the Oslo problem when you put it together.

Warm, little, smooth-fitting caps that match a sweater take the raw edge off the wind-chill factor. They also hide the effect of winter static electricity on hair. Use a yarn that is not scratchy and that makes a springy ribbing.

Measure, calculate, draft, and knit. Measure around your head at eyebrow level. Add 2" for comfort. That is the circumference of your cap.

Measure from your eyebrows to the top of your head. Add 1½" for sewing and cutting. That is the length of your cap.

Convert the inches to stitches and rows, and you have the draft for your cap: a rectangle.

Knit it. Rib the bottom 1½". Do not bother to cast off the top. Full the cap, fix the glitches, and press the fabric.

Sew. Sew the ends of the rectangle together wrong side out, to make a circle. Keep the seam right at the edges of the fabric. Make two darts by sewing shaping seams. The darts should take in one-eighth of the width of the cap, and then should taper off halfway down its length. It doesn't seem to matter whether the darts are straight or curved; the knitting will stretch to accommodate your head. Trim off the extra fabric.

Pin the two darts together. Sew two more darts at the sides. Trim off the extra fabric.

Pin the four darts into two pairs. Sew two more darts at the sides, making their top points meet. If there's a gap at the top of the darts, you will need to fix a hole at the top of your cap. Trim off the extra fabric.

Pin the two sets of three darts together, and sew the last two darts. Try to make all the darts connect at the top. There's a lot of knitting bundled in there, so be careful how you pin and sew. It's easy to break your sewing machine needle over that hump. Trim off the last of the extra fabric.

Turn the cap right side out, and press all the seams flat.

Measurements for a cap

	Body	Adjustment (for ease, cutting, and seams)	Adjusted measurement
Around the head	____"	+ 2"	____"
Brow to crown	____"	+ 1½"	____"

Measurements for a close-fitting cap

Measure all around the head and add 2". This is the width of the fabric for your cap.

Measure from eyebrows to crown of head and add 1½". This is the length of the fabric for your cap.

Design a cap

If you're putting in patterns and stripes, keep them in the lower half, or they'll get lost in the shaping.

don't bother binding off

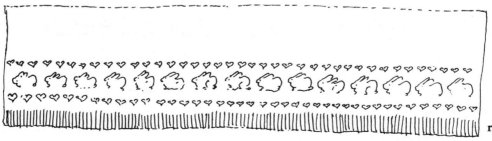

ribbing

A cap in inches

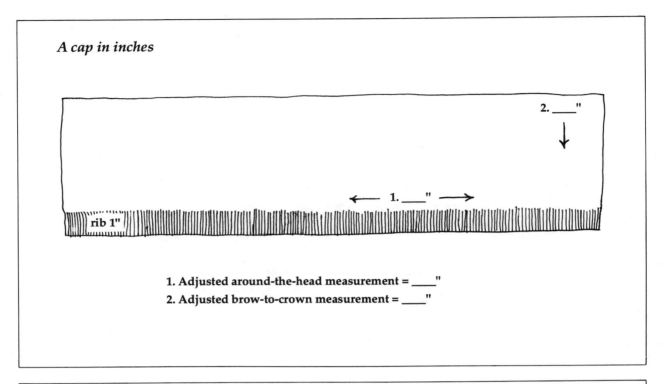

1. Adjusted around-the-head measurement = ____"
2. Adjusted brow-to-crown measurement = ____"

A cap in stitches and rows

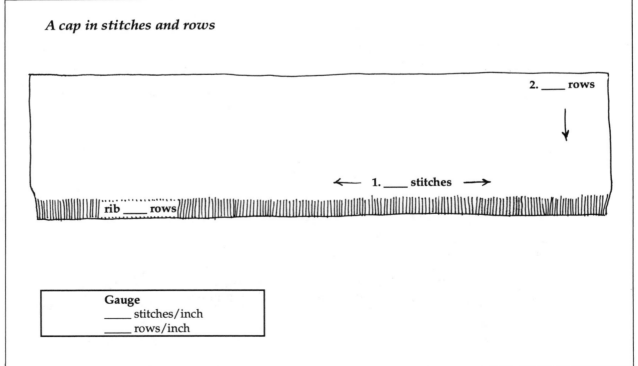

Gauge
____ stitches/inch
____ rows/inch

Putting together a cap

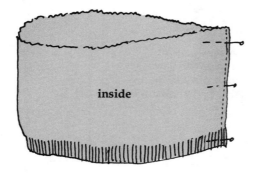

1. Sew the rectangle into a cylinder, using the narrowest possible seam allowance.

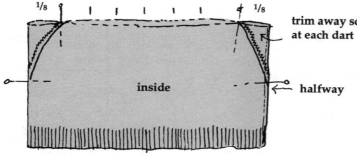

2. Zigzag darts at each side; each dart should use up ⅛ of the width of the folded fabric and ½ of its length. If the darts look right, sew the seams with a straight stitch and trim away the extra fabric.

trim away scrap at each dart

halfway

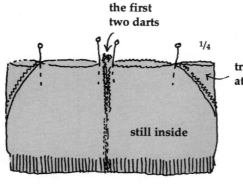

the first two darts

trim away scrap at each dart

3. Pin those two seams together, and sew two more. Trim the extra fabric.

get the darts to meet at a point

trim

4. Pin together two new pairs of darts—one in each pair will have been sewn in step 2 and one in step 3—and sew two more darts. Trim the extra fabric.

There's a lot here to sew. Be careful to not break your needle.

trim

inside, still

5. Pin all the darts together in the center, and make your last two darts go across the top of the cap.

A cap is easy to press if you fit it over a rolled-up towel

If there's a gap here, fix it by hand.

right side out

6. Turn the cap right side out. All the seams should meet at the top. Press the seams.

Berets

Berets are for days when you want to look jaunty and bohemian. They are also for days when you do not want to deal with your hair. A floppy beret can disguise a disappointing perm, or Thursday before the hairdresser, or the effects of a rough round of chemotherapy. A very large beret can bundle up a whole mane of dreadlocks, or keep romantic tresses out of heavy machinery or someone's dinner.

Berets succeed with floppy knits, like silk or cotton. They need to be pattable and smooshable, so you can sculpt them a bit when you wear them.

Calculate, draft, knit, and sew. Knit a beret 6" or more wider than your head's circumference. The full width of your knitting machine may do nicely. Knit it 6" or more longer than the measurement from your brow to your crown. Don't bother with ribbing; just cast on and knit. Don't bother to bind off.

Full, fix, and press the fabric. Sew the beret into a cylinder and make darts in its top, in the same way that you would begin a cap.

Finish. When you've got the dome of the beret all darted, turn under the bottom edge of the fabric as if you were going to sew a ½" hem. Sew it in place all the way around, but stop ¼" shy of the end. Slip a bodkin with soft ¼" elastic into this casing. The length of the elastic should be the same as the circumference of your head. When the elastic is all through the casing, sew it into a circle and close the gap in the hem.

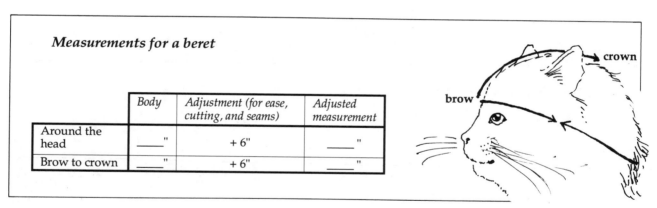

Measurements for a beret

	Body	Adjustment (for ease, cutting, and seams)	Adjusted measurement
Around the head	____"	+ 6"	____"
Brow to crown	____"	+ 6"	____"

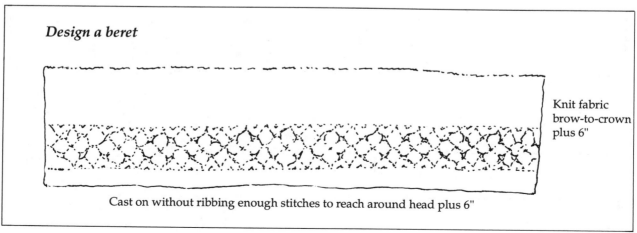

Design a beret

Knit fabric brow-to-crown plus 6"

Cast on without ribbing enough stitches to reach around head plus 6"

157

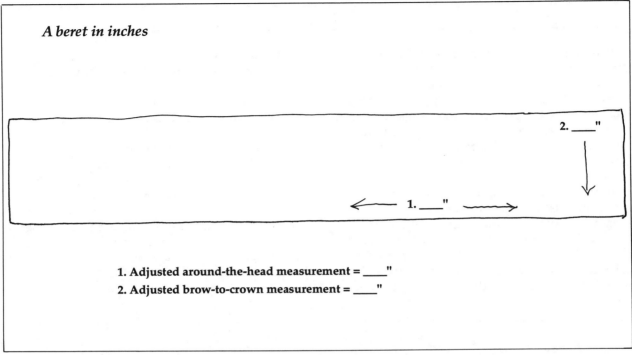

A beret in inches

1. Adjusted around-the-head measurement = ____"
2. Adjusted brow-to-crown measurement = ____"

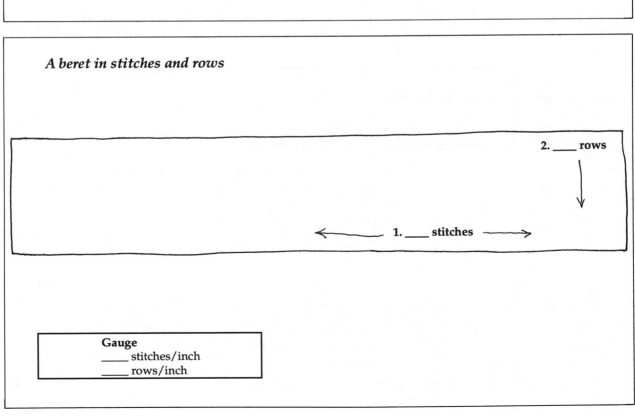

A beret in stitches and rows

Gauge
____ stitches/inch
____ rows/inch

Putting together a beret

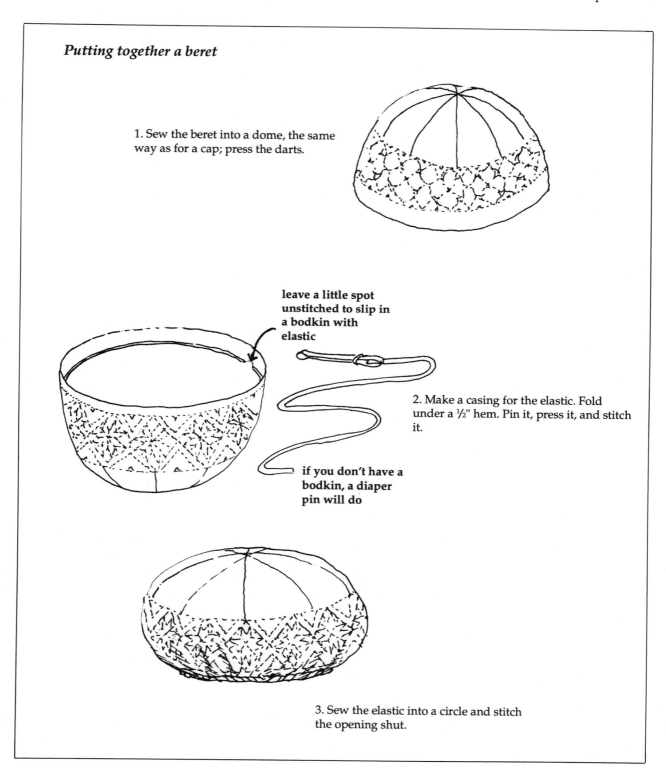

1. Sew the beret into a dome, the same way as for a cap; press the darts.

leave a little spot unstitched to slip in a bodkin with elastic

if you don't have a bodkin, a diaper pin will do

2. Make a casing for the elastic. Fold under a ½" hem. Pin it, press it, and stitch it.

3. Sew the elastic into a circle and stitch the opening shut.

Mittens & Gloves

Mittens

Some people know and love mittens; some disdain them, preferring gloves. Mitten people are found waiting for buses at -20° F, shoveling drifts of snow from driveways, mushing malamutes, chopping stovewood before the blizzard hits, and cross-country skiing. People who love mittens do so because everything else leaves their fingers aching from the cold. Mittens keep your hands *warm*.

Look through your test swatches for a wool trial that seemed too dense to make a great sweater. Fair Isle patterning is useful, because it makes a double layer of yarn. When you do a gauge test for wool mittens, try fulling it in warmer water and with more agitation than you would use for a sweater. A thick, dense knit makes a warmer, tougher mitten.

Design. Trace around your hand on a piece of paper. That is your mitten design. Draw in initials, critters, stripes, whatever you found promising in the test and gauge swatches.

Calculate, draft, and knit. You're going to knit both mittens in one piece, and cut them apart later. The thumbs are separate. The mittens piece will be a rectangle. There should be at least 3" of ribbing at the bottom, to warm your wrists and keep the blizzard from getting up your sleeves.

The hand part of the mitten is the length of your hand from the fold line at your wrist to the tip of your longest finger, plus 1" for shaping, sewing, and cutting. This measurement plus the ribbing is the length of the mittens piece.

Measure around your hand where it's widest. Add 1" for sewing and cutting. This is the width of one mitten piece. Since you're knitting both at once, double that to get the width of the mittens piece.

Some mittens have the thumb added as a tubular bit that grows out of the palm of the mitten. Palm readers would be dismayed to see a thumb folded back into a hand like that; it would be read as depression and listlessness. Palmists prefer that thumbs spring away from the side of the hand, indicating energy, intelligence, and joy. Thus the thumb pieces for these mittens will be knitted and

sewn into the side seams of the mittens in a way that pleases palmists, and is also most useful for gripping ski poles, doorknobs, and ax handles.

Calculate the thumb pieces as follows. Measure around your thumb, and add 1" for seaming, shaping, and flexibility. That is the width of the top part of the thumb piece.

Measure from your thumb's tip to the crease that separates it from your palm. That will be the length of the top part of the thumb piece.

The bottom part of the thumb piece is a triangle of 2 stitches cast on, increased a stitch on each side every other row, until you reach the width of the top half.

After you've calculated the thumbs pieces and the mittens piece, draft them according to the gauge of your more-fulled-than-usual swatch.

Knit the mittens piece and the thumbs, then full and press them.

Sew. Chalk a line down the middle of the mittens piece, and zigzag on either side of it. Cut the mittens apart. Put your hand on one of the mitten pieces, to see where the thumb piece should be set. Chalk that.

Pin one triangular part of the thumb piece to the edge of the mitten in the chalked spot. Sew it on with a very narrow seam. Pin the other increasing side to the other side of the mitten, and pin the wrist ribbing below the thumb together, too. Sew that seam close to the edge.

Fold over the hand part of the mitten and pin it. Put your hand in place on the mitten, and chalk a curved line over your fingers where the mitten seam should be. Chalk a little arc where your thumb comes to a tip. Zigzag over those chalk lines. Sew a seam just under the finger zigzag, and sew on around to just under the thumb zigzag. Trim off the extra fabric, keeping close to the zigzag (especially at the thumb). Turn the mitten right side out.

Heat up your iron and get it full of steam. As you press the mitten, pinch, poke, and pull the curved seams into shape. This will take some determination, but the wool will respond to the effort (if you've knit your mittens with acrylic, it will just sit there).

Sew up the other mitten in the same way, if your hands are the same.

If your hands are not identical. Some people are born missing bits and pieces, others lose parts along the way. If it's your hands that got rear-

ranged, and you would prefer that both mittens fit, rather than one going floppy, you'll need different drafts.

But there's a bonus hidden in this situation. Two pairs of mittens are useful. Calculate one pair from one hand, and one pair from the other. Two different pairs of mittens become . . . two pairs of different mittens!

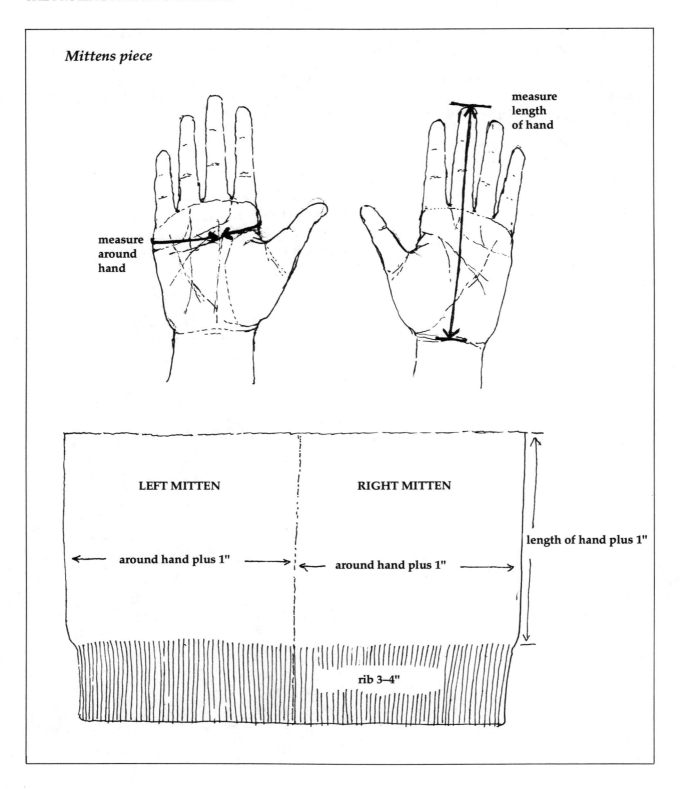

Mittens piece

measure length of hand

measure around hand

LEFT MITTEN

RIGHT MITTEN

length of hand plus 1"

← around hand plus 1" →

← around hand plus 1" →

rib 3–4"

Thumb piece

Make 2.

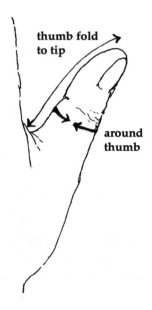

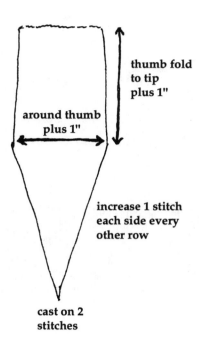

thumb fold to tip

around thumb

thumb fold to tip plus 1"

around thumb plus 1"

increase 1 stitch each side every other row

cast on 2 stitches

Measurements for mittens

	Body	Adjustment (for ease, cutting, and seams)	Adjusted measurement
Around hand	____ "	+ 1"	____ "
Length of hand	____ "	+ 1"	____ "
Around thumb	____ "	+ 1"	____ "
Thumb fold to tip	____ "	+ 1"	____ "

Mittens in inches

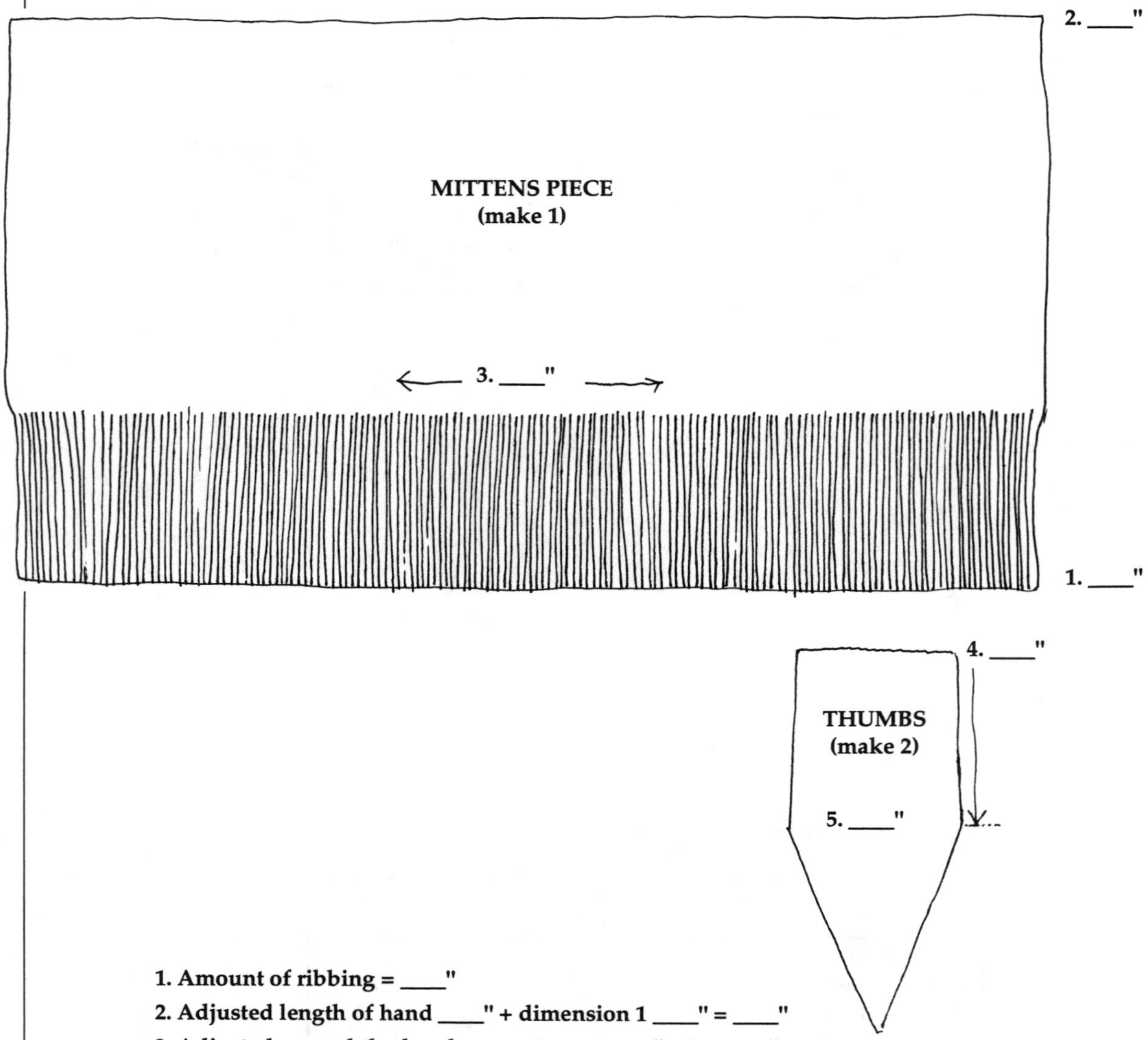

2. ____"

MITTENS PIECE
(make 1)

← 3. ____" →

1. ____"

4. ____"

THUMBS
(make 2)

5. ____"

1. Amount of ribbing = ____"
2. Adjusted length of hand ____" + dimension 1 ____" = ____"
3. Adjusted around-the-hand measurement ____" × 2 = ____"
4. Adjusted tip-to-crease thumb measurement = ____"
5. Adjusted thumb-width measurement = ____"

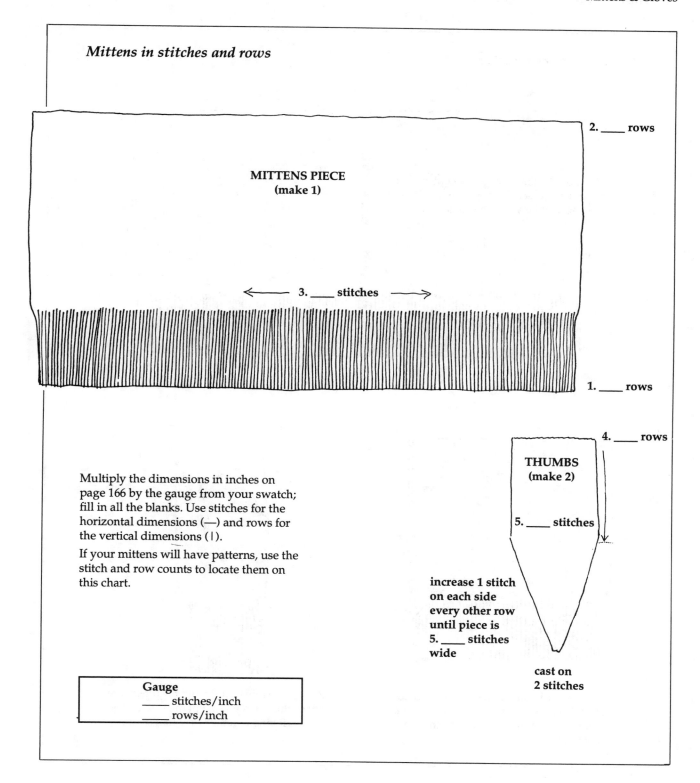

Mittens in stitches and rows

MITTENS PIECE
(make 1)

2. ____ rows

←——— 3. ____ stitches ———→

1. ____ rows

4. ____ rows

THUMBS
(make 2)

5. ____ stitches

Multiply the dimensions in inches on page 166 by the gauge from your swatch; fill in all the blanks. Use stitches for the horizontal dimensions (—) and rows for the vertical dimensions (|).

If your mittens will have patterns, use the stitch and row counts to locate them on this chart.

increase 1 stitch on each side every other row until piece is 5. ____ stitches wide

cast on 2 stitches

Gauge
____ stitches/inch
____ rows/inch

167

Putting mittens together

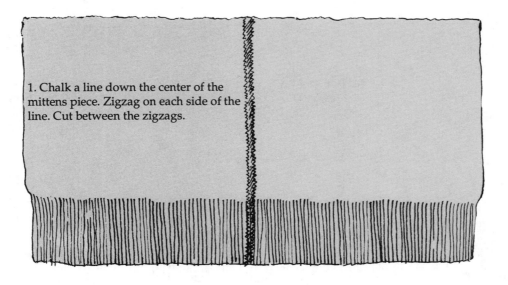

1. Chalk a line down the center of the mittens piece. Zigzag on each side of the line. Cut between the zigzags.

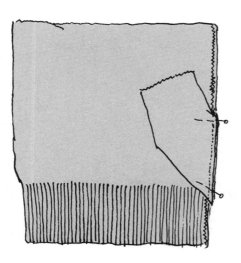

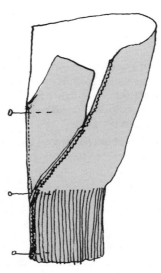

2. Put your hand on one mitten piece to see where the thumb should go. Pin one angled side of the thumb piece there. Sew that seam.

3. Fold the mitten over; pin the other side of the thumb in place. Pin the side edges of the ribbing together. Sew that seam.

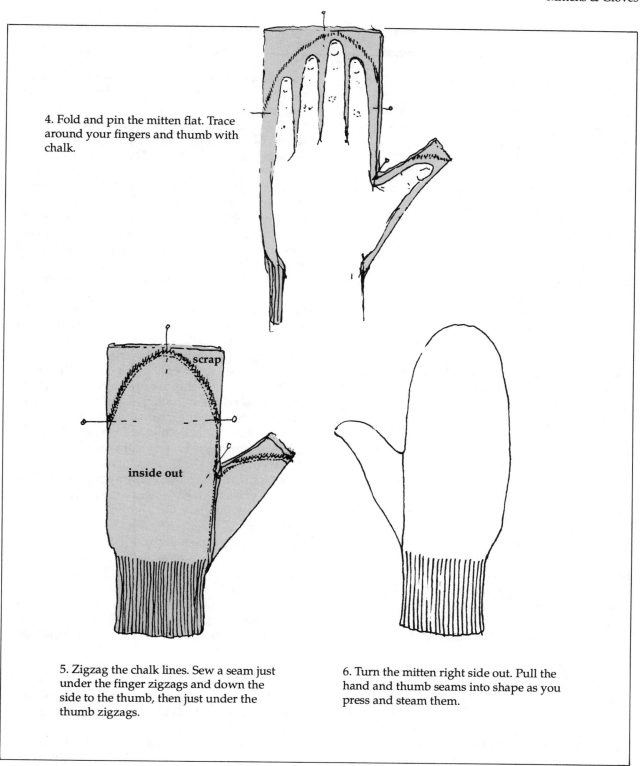

4. Fold and pin the mitten flat. Trace around your fingers and thumb with chalk.

scrap

inside out

5. Zigzag the chalk lines. Sew a seam just under the finger zigzags and down the side to the thumb, then just under the thumb zigzags.

6. Turn the mitten right side out. Pull the hand and thumb seams into shape as you press and steam them.

Gloves

Household knitting machines were not born to make gloves. There are industrial circular machines that handle the job well, but your device will need to be coaxed. Getting your knitting machine to make gloves is like teaching a cat to bark: with guile, you'll succeed.

Industrial machines, however, are strongly biased toward people with ten unexceptional fingers. The barking-cat glove method has the advantage that it does not play favorites. It accommodates people with two fingers, fourteen, or any other array. It also allows you to leave fingertips or whole fingers unsheathed. If you need gloves that let you count change, bait an ice-fishing hook, play pennywhistle, or jump start a truck in the snow, you can knit a pair to suit the business at hand.

Because barking-cat gloves require smooth grafts, you will need to have developed some cleverness in that respect. You can quickly get several pairs off the machine, but it will take time to sew them up. For each glove, plan on one rerun or one lazy lunch hour.

Design. Trace around your hands. Decide whether you want any fingertips open; draw them in. Decide if you want to knit a pattern in; draw that. This is your design.

Find a knitting swatch that is both warm and supple, because gloves need to be flexible. Get a *very* accurate gauge from your test piece—gloves must fit "like a glove."

Calculate and draft. Measure around your palm; that is the width of a hand piece. Measure from the crease where your wrist bends to the place where your fingers start; that is the length of a hand piece. There will be 3" to 4" of ribbing in addition to this length.

The glove fingers will be knitted all in one long piece, then cut into lengths and assembled. Measure around each of your fingers. If they're nearly the same, you can knit the fingers piece all at that one width. Measure the length of every finger, and add the results together. Add as many inches for cutting and fiddling as you have fingers. That is the length of the fingers piece. If your fingers differ by ½" or more in circumference, knit the fingers

piece to the smaller dimension first, as long as you need to cover the small fingers, then increase to the larger diameter.

The thumb pieces are separate. Measure the length of your thumb, from its tip to the crease that divides it from your hand. That is the length of the top part of each thumb piece. Measure around your thumb. That is the width of the top part of each thumb piece. The bottom part of the thumb piece is a triangle, begun with two cast-on stitches and increased one stitch each side on every other row until it is as wide as the top part of the thumb piece.

If your hands are very different—for example, you have five fingers on one hand and three and a half on the other—draft each glove separately. If the needs of your hands are different from each other—for example, you play a trumpet at a snowy forty-yard line and need three right-hand fingertips bare, the rest covered—you can do the same.

When all the inches are noted in your calculations, convert them to stitches and rows, using the numbers from your gauge sample.

Knit. Knit the hand pieces. Instead of binding off their top edges, knit an extra three rows in scrap yarn.

Knit the thumb pieces, and work an extra 1" at the top of each so that you can ravel back when you are sewing them on. This will help you get a perfect fit.

If your machine will make a tube, knit the fingers piece as one long tube. If it won't, make a long strip. You'll sew each finger into a tube as you attach it to the hand.

Full all the pieces, and press everything flat. It is important that your glove pieces be humble and cooperative as you do the sewing, so use plenty of steam and press thoroughly.

Sew. This whole section consists of hand sewing, with the same yarn you used for knitting—literally! You'll unravel part of each piece to obtain the sewing strand. As you adjust each bit, press the unraveled yarn smooth and then thread it into your needle. This eliminates a few loose ends.

Put your hand on the hand piece, and position

Figure out a glove

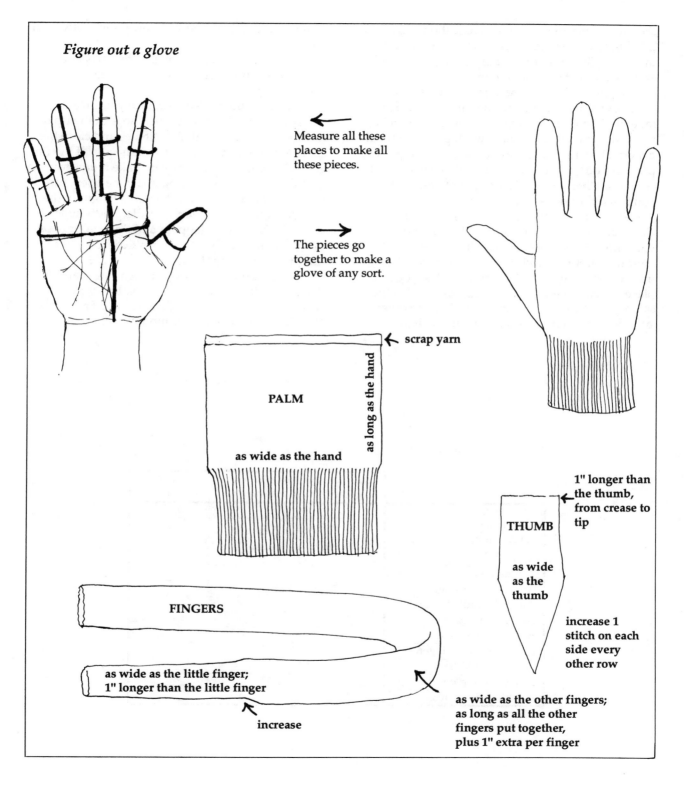

Measure all these places to make all these pieces.

The pieces go together to make a glove of any sort.

← scrap yarn

PALM

as long as the hand

as wide as the hand

THUMB

1" longer than the thumb, from crease to tip

as wide as the thumb

increase 1 stitch on each side every other row

FINGERS

as wide as the little finger; 1" longer than the little finger

increase

as wide as the other fingers; as long as all the other fingers put together, plus 1" extra per finger

the thumb increasing part where it should go. Sew the thumb on there, then sew it to the other side of the hand piece. Join the ribbing below the thumb, and the hand above the thumb.

How many stitches are there around the hand? And how many stitches around all the fingers put together? You'll find there are a few more stitches in the fingers; these will be sewn together in the finger crotches. Remember as you sew the fingers on the hand how many stitches should be reserved for crotches, otherwise you'll run out of hand before you run out of fingers.

Gently unravel the scrap yarn from the hand. Cut a length of the fingers piece 1" longer than your index finger, and unravel it two rows at the bottom. Careful handling will keep the stitches from unraveling farther. Graft the index finger in place, leaving the crotch stitches unsewn. Do the same with the pinky finger, then fill in the other fingers. Sew their crotches together. If the fingers weren't knitted in tube-form, sew them halfway up now.

Put your hand in the glove. If the tip is to be sewn closed, unravel the index finger to just over the fingertip.

Thread the unraveled yarn into your needle, and run the needle through the loops at the tip of the finger. Gather up all the stitches and close the circle with a stitch or two of your needle. If the finger isn't completely a tube yet, make it one now.

If the tip of the glove finger is to be open, unravel it as far as suits you. Thread a length of the unraveled thread into your needle. Buttonhole stitch through every loop, to make a firm edge on the glove finger. If the finger isn't completely a tube, finish making it one.

Go through this process for each finger and for the thumb. If you go about this patiently, no one will ever know that your glove came off a home machine and not a trickier model.

Measurements for gloves

	Body	Adjustment (for ease, cutting, and seams)	Adjusted measurement
Around hand	____"		
Length of palm (wrist crease to start of fingers)	____"		
Around thumb	____"		
Thumb fold to tip	____"	+ 1"	____"
Around index finger	____"		
Around middle finger	____"		
Around ring finger	____"		
Around little finger	____"		
Length of index finger	____"	+ 1"	____"
Length of middle finger	____"	+ 1"	____"
Length of ring finger	____"	+ 1"	____"
Length of little finger	____"	+ 1"	____"

A glove in inches

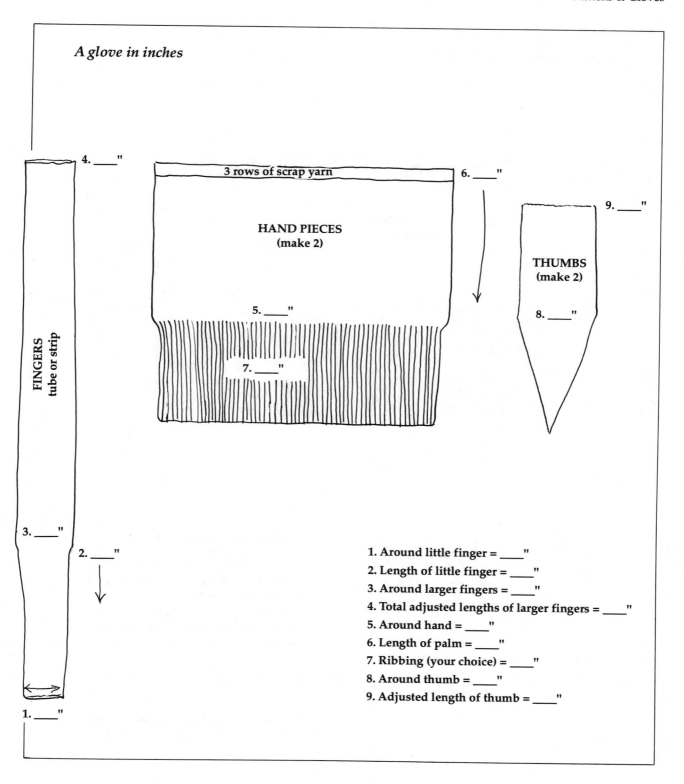

FINGERS
tube or strip

4. _____"

3 rows of scrap yarn

6. _____"

HAND PIECES
(make 2)

THUMBS
(make 2)

9. _____"

5. _____"

8. _____"

7. _____"

3. _____"

2. _____"

1. _____"

1. **Around little finger** = _____"
2. **Length of little finger** = _____"
3. **Around larger fingers** = _____"
4. **Total adjusted lengths of larger fingers** = _____"
5. **Around hand** = _____"
6. **Length of palm** = _____"
7. **Ribbing (your choice)** = _____"
8. **Around thumb** = _____"
9. **Adjusted length of thumb** = _____"

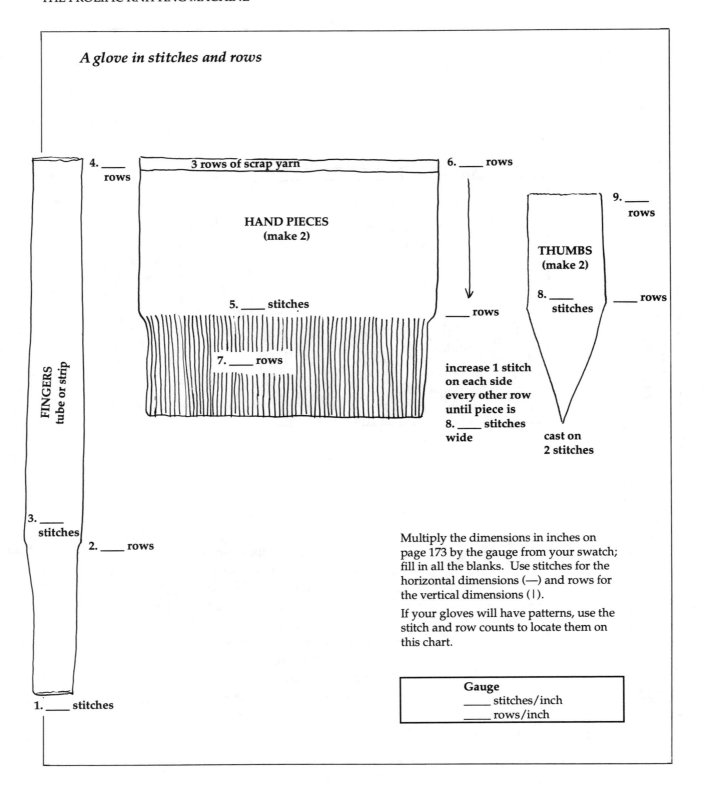

A glove in stitches and rows

4. _____ rows

3 rows of scrap yarn

6. _____ rows

HAND PIECES
(make 2)

9. _____ rows

THUMBS
(make 2)

5. _____ stitches

_____ rows

8. _____ stitches

_____ rows

FINGERS
tube or strip

7. _____ rows

increase 1 stitch
on each side
every other row
until piece is
8. _____ stitches
wide

cast on
2 stitches

3. _____ stitches

2. _____ rows

1. _____ stitches

Multiply the dimensions in inches on
page 173 by the gauge from your swatch;
fill in all the blanks. Use stitches for the
horizontal dimensions (—) and rows for
the vertical dimensions (|).

If your gloves will have patterns, use the
stitch and row counts to locate them on
this chart.

Gauge
_____ stitches/inch
_____ rows/inch

Putting a glove together

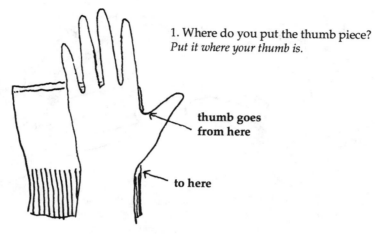

1. Where do you put the thumb piece?
Put it where your thumb is.

**thumb goes
from here**

to here

2. Hand sew one angled side of the
thumb into place on one side of the palm.
Fold the palm around to sew the other V
side of the thumb. Sew the ribbing seam.
Sew the thumb crotch seam.

waste rows

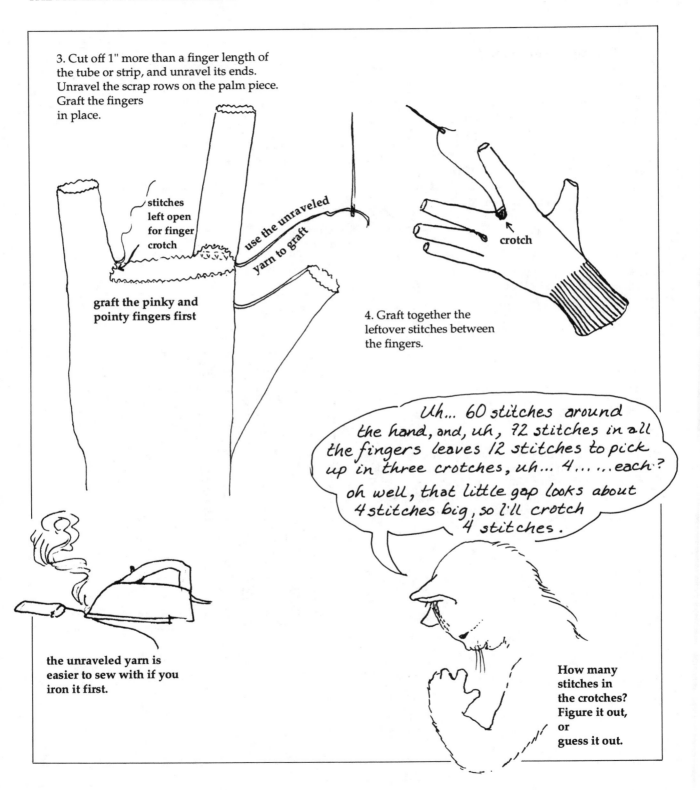

3. Cut off 1" more than a finger length of the tube or strip, and unravel its ends. Unravel the scrap rows on the palm piece. Graft the fingers in place.

stitches left open for finger crotch

use the unraveled yarn to graft

graft the pinky and pointy fingers first

crotch

4. Graft together the leftover stitches between the fingers.

Uh... 60 stitches around the hand, and, uh, 72 stitches in all the fingers leaves 12 stitches to pick up in three crotches, uh... 4.......each?

oh well, that little gap looks about 4 stitches big, so I'll crotch 4 stitches.

the unraveled yarn is easier to sew with if you iron it first.

How many stitches in the crotches? Figure it out, or guess it out.

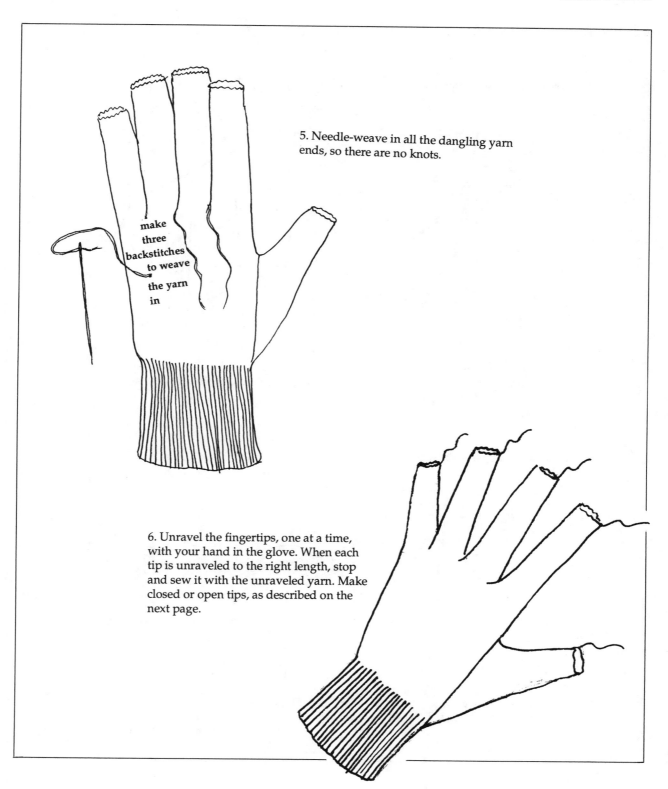

make three backstitches to weave the yarn in

5. Needle-weave in all the dangling yarn ends, so there are no knots.

6. Unravel the fingertips, one at a time, with your hand in the glove. When each tip is unraveled to the right length, stop and sew it with the unraveled yarn. Make closed or open tips, as described on the next page.

7. To make a closed fingertip:

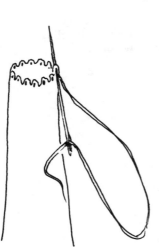
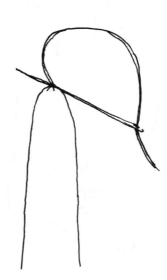

Thread yarn
through all the
unraveled loops.

Pull them tight.

Stitch the tip closed.

8. To make an open fingertip:

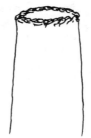

Unravel to a
likely spot.

Work around the
opening,

securing each
loop with a
buttonhole stitch.

Any combination of short, long, closed, or
open fingers is possible.

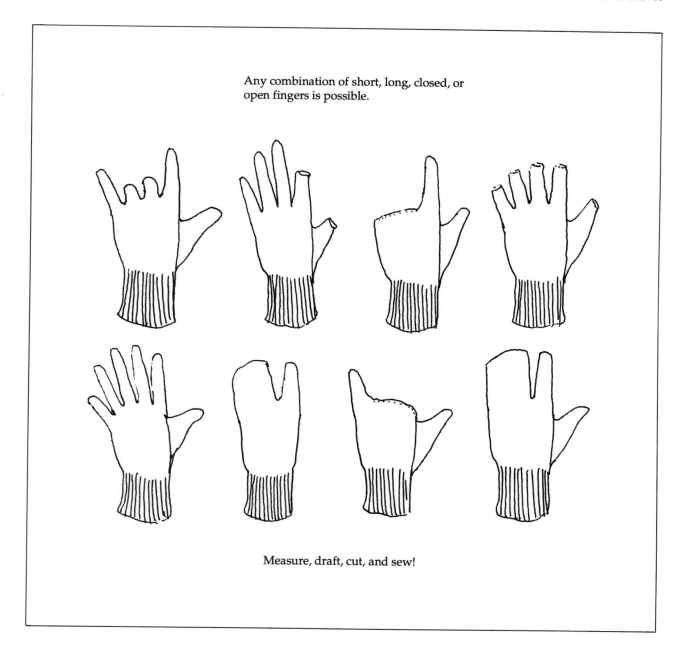

Measure, draft, cut, and sew!

When Nothing Goes Right

The weapons of war

Needle-nose pliers will get jammed needles out of your machine; they will also get the wire in and out of the cast-on comb.

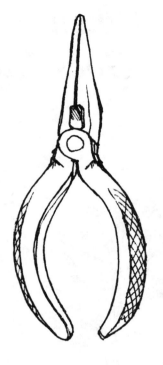

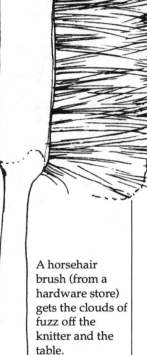

Transparent tape will pick barely visible but disastrous crud out of tight spots in the computer.

A horsehair brush (from a hardware store) gets the clouds of fuzz off the knitter and the table.

A bit of rag will wipe out the lumps of grease, fuzz, and metal-wear from the machine's carriage and from the tracks the carriage runs along.

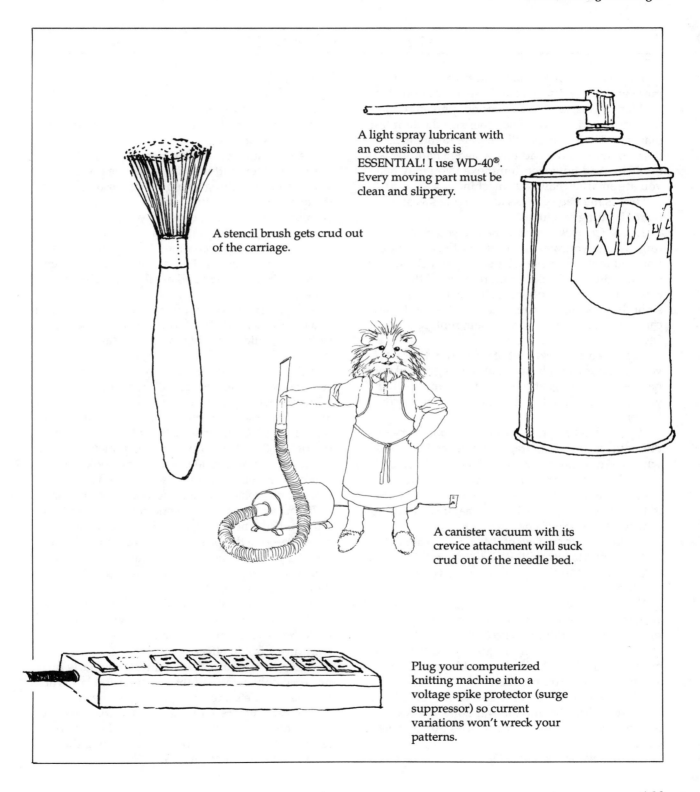

A light spray lubricant with an extension tube is ESSENTIAL! I use WD-40®. Every moving part must be clean and slippery.

A stencil brush gets crud out of the carriage.

A canister vacuum with its crevice attachment will suck crud out of the needle bed.

Plug your computerized knitting machine into a voltage spike protector (surge suppressor) so current variations won't wreck your patterns.

When Nothing Goes Right

The more complex your knitting machine, the more varied the disasters and the more subtle the problems. This, of course, does not prevent you from discovering a wretched mess on the simplest machine. These things *will* happen. Remember that, no matter how bad it is, a sledge hammer will not help. And however flummoxed you may be, you are smarter than your machine.

Here is my bag of tricks for coaxing sweaters out of knitting machines.

1. *Look for crooked needles.* Before you start knitting, pull all your needles to the farthest-out position and look for ones that are not parallel. Slide all the straight ones back in, and remove all the crooked ones. Look down each one, like you'd sight down a billiard cue, and straighten it, if you can. If the needle is beyond repair, replace it with a fresh one.

Bent needles cause a lot of grief. Any time you're knitting and hear the ominous *grunnnkt* of a needle being bent, get the turkey out and fix it. If you don't, it will only get worse and foul up your knitting.

If yarn is getting hung up in one spot every row, piling up or splitting, drag out that needle and see what's wrong. Sometimes the latch will have been pushed crooked, or the hook will have gotten un-bent, or the needle may resemble the letter W. Fix it. If the needle is so badly bent that it won't come out, gentle it out with needle-nose pliers.

2. *Clean all the crud out of the carriage.* Then zap all the movable bits with WD-40®. If you do this before you start knitting, you may save yourself much profanity.

When something is obviously going wrong while you're knitting and a bent needle isn't the problem, the first thing to do is clean and lube the carriage works. That will frequently free up whatever was sticking. The brushes sold for stenciling are my favorite crud brushes.

When your carriage jams and won't come loose, blast some WD-40® into the war zone and wait a few minutes. This always persuades things to let go for me.

3. *Clean all the fuzz out of the machine's computer, if*
it has one. One of my machines needs to be defuzzed daily, or it does unsavory things to patterns. Another tolerates a month's fuzz before it gets cranky. A small soft brush does a fair job, but a slip of transparent tape works better.

If something peculiar happens to the pattern on your computer knitter and you're sure it wasn't your fault, try putting a surge suppressor between the outlet and your plug. Variations in household current—which can be caused by appliances which automatically switch off and on—can zap your computer. In fact, I recommend that you get one of these sanity preservers before you have a problem. They don't cost much, and are found at electronics stores.

4. *Try different yarn.* Sometimes one skein of yarn in a bundle is recalcitrant. Any basic nastiness in the yarn would have shown up on a sample swatch.

5. *Observe your machine in slow motion.* Are you convinced that there is something really wrong with the machine's mechanics? Peer into the levers and slidy parts under the carriage. Click all the buttons slowly. Watch for something that's not moving right; a lot of the stuff works symmetrically, so watch for asymmetrical movements. Look for stuck levers (blast with WD-40®) and floppy ones (they have broken springs and need to be repaired).

If you see what's wrong and think you could fix it if you had a new part, try calling the manufacturer. Describe the problem and see if they'll send you the piece you need. You can also try this with your dealer/repairman; mine has cooperated wonderfully in this regard.

If you find a broken part that you absolutely cannot (or don't dare to) fix yourself, sigh deeply and pack the machine off for repair. Maybe your warranty's still in effect.

6. *Check the tension.* If the knitting regularly but unexpectedly comes off the machine and lands at your feet, there's a tension problem somewhere.

The yarn may be looping up under the carriage between rows, which produces a sudden lack of tension. You can fix this by gently stroking the yarn up at the end of each row.

Train your ears and hands to tell you if the knitting's going to hit the floor before your eyes see it happening. The knitting will "sound wrong," or you will feel the carriage move differently. Stay alert and don't knit too fast, and you'll drop only a few stitches and not a whole row.

7. Send all children, spouses, lovers, and onlookers out of the room. This can help if you've straightened, cleaned, inspected, unsurged, and made sure everything is in working order, but you are still getting blunder after blunder.

Some knitting machines are shy and foul up when watched. Perhaps you are shy or distracted, and small lapses in concentration are turning into bungles. Either my knitting machine is very jealous and can't bear for me to pay attention to anything else, or I have to be in a state of peaceful attentiveness to get everything right. In either case, solitude is the cure.

Are you tired? Worried? You need to be relaxed and alert to keep track of your knitting. Some medi-cations that make you jittery or dull-witted will cause you hours of extra work, fixing all the mistakes.

8. Try again later. If everything's functional, and you're alone and in a gently productive mood, and you've still knitted a woolly disaster . . . go relax and have a cup of tea. The moon must be void of course, or Mercury is in retrograde, or the phone is about to ring. Maybe when you return after a break the problem will have cured itself, or its solution will bubble up out of your unconscious.

9. Try unsensible things. When everything sensible fails, be inventive. If you have a Japanese machine, burn incense for it, and lay out rice wine and tangerines to appease its malevolent spirit. I suppose a Swiss machine could be wooed with chocolates and classical music. Make up a ritual of cleansing and blessing for your machine; scatter a little salt around on the floor. These practices won't hurt a thing, and you can always drink the wine or eat the chocolates yourself.

Appendix

Handspinning for your knitting machine

Is your spinning wheel a better therapist for you than a Jungian analyst? Does spinning improve your outlook on life more than two self-help books? Does spinning calm you more than three trips to the hot tub? Do you have enough magnificent handspun yarn on hand to make Rumpelstiltskin an offer he can't refuse? If you are a natural-born spinning wizard, your knitting machine can be your next-best friend.

Some machines are broad-minded and will knit up medium-weight handspun yarns with ease. The yarns do need to be free of lumps, loops, and weak spots, and I strongly recommend using plied yarn so the knitted pieces won't skew out of shape. If you have a bulky machine and it doesn't seem to be very picky about the yarn you feed it, simply try out any handspun you've got that looks appropriate.

The key to handspinning for any knitting machine, bulky or fine, is to examine the yarns your machine loves and to imitate them. Try out a small swatch. If it works, try a bigger one. As long as you can spin a large enough quantity of yarn at a consistent gauge, any garment in this book can be done in handspun. If you're a spinner, I don't have to explain why handspun yarn is worth the effort.

If your machine uses the finer gauges of yarn—2/6, 2/7, 2/8, and such—you may be daunted at the prospect of using your own yarn. Don't panic, though. I've knitted several garments of handspun. My yarn was a two-ply of about 1600 yards per pound, and spinning to this gauge wasn't particularly difficult once I got the hang of it. The only hard part was in shifting my time frame. Where I used to fill a bobbin in 20 minutes (with 50 yards, or one ounce, of singles yarn), I needed to plan on filling one in four hours (with 400 yards, or two ounces, of singles yarn). I suggest that you rent movies you've wanted to see and park your wheel in front of the VCR. (Or see if your library has audiotapes of someone reading *Anna Karenina*.) You should be able to spin enough for a sweater in about 25 movies. Rent some more for the plying.

Therefore, have a look at your knitting machine and at a commercial yarn that gives you no trouble whatsoever. Ask yourself, "Can I duplicate this yarn?"

If you answer, "Of course I can! I've already got a closet bursting with immaculate, fine, plied skeins," fantastic. Match up skeins by texture and gauge, cast on and knit up test swatches, and make that avalanche of yarn leap into garments. Just skim this section so you can avoid trouble.

If you answer, "I think I can—if I have the right fleece and a little practice," then get comfortable and read this section a couple of times. Handspinning for a knitting machine isn't difficult for an experienced spinner, but it's most troublefree if some parts are done exactly right, without shortcuts.

Here are a few more sober questions before you get ambitious. Do you love spinning enough to spend twenty hours at the wheel for each hour at the knitting machine? Are you comfortable putting seventy hours of labor into a sweater? Can you keep an even spinning gauge for enough yarn to make the whole sweater? Can you do this on your existing schedule?

Can you spin a yarn which is precisely even? Lumps can catch in the carriage and break the yarn. Then the knitting will land at your feet. A thin spot can give way in the hooks, and your knitting will have a great hole.

The only real difficulty of spinning for a knitting machine is maintaining an even thickness for a whole sweater's worth of yarn. If that much immaculate spinning seems impossible, consider making caps and mittens, or a vest.

Go back to your machine's favorite yarn. What qualities does your machine love most? The yarn is springy; it gives a bit as each hook pulls it, and then puffs back a little to make a well-filled-out stitch. Fine wool is the most foolproof material from which to make such a yarn; I recommend wool with a tight crimp for its springiness. If you feel you must use a straight fiber, blend it with a crimpy one. And if your machine tolerates cotton or silk well, try spinning a two-ply yarn at the correct weight and see how it goes. But I suggest you begin with wool.

Spinning thin, even, strong yarn isn't difficult if

your fleece has been properly prepared. The more perfect the carding or combing, the more even the spinning. Machines do a very thorough job of cleaning and sorting fleece. If you find wool preparation tedious, buy the prettified stuff; there's no sin in it. Buy twice as much sliver or carded wool by weight as you would yarn for a similar project; this will give you margin for waste and error (or surplus for hats and mittens).

If you can purchase wool in the form of sliver or roving, you will acquire a tidy rope of clean fiber to spin from. Pluck off 6" of the sliver or roving, wrap it around your fingers, and spin away. If you can purchase clean carded fleece, you'll have no difficulty with that, either.

If you love the earthy magnificence of a whole, raw fleece unrolled on your workroom floor, and you adore the pungent smell, and you enjoy releasing the opalescent fibers from their rich oils, and you *must* do every step yourself, here's how. Go find a Merino, or Merino cross, or Rambouillet, or other very fine-wooled beast, and inquire about its

How do you know if your handspun will work? Knit a 3"x 3" trial.... if a little works, a lot will. Fine wool isn't the only thing you can use, it's just the most foolproof. Try stuff!

pasturage and health. If the creature was well-fed all year, is young and healthy, suffered no drought or heat stress, and managed not to wallow in either prickles or mud, buy its fleece.

If you are instead perusing fleeces in a shop, pluck out a lock from the one that catches your fancy and examine it carefully. You want a lot of little crimps, not a few deep waves. A long staple is better than a short one. Tug at the lock hard; strong fleece indicates that the sheep was healthy and your yarn will be glossy, sturdy, and even. Poor quality fleece makes ratty, weak yarn.

Skirt your fleece—that is, remove all the short, dirty, crummy wool around the edges. You must work with only the best of the fleece. Including the short bits will only give you lumps and pills.

Clean the fleece. Dishwashing liquids that can handle baked-on lasagna do a good job on fleeces. Run warm water in your sink and be generous with the dish detergent. Add half a sinkful of wool, smooshing it gently to loosen the dirt; try not to disturb the structure of the locks. Drain and rinse

twice. Go through this process eight or so times. Rinse a few more times, pressing the wool to see if any dirt or grease remains.

Roll the clean wet wool in a towel, and do a little dance on the towel to press out the water. Lay the clean, moist wool on a fresh towel to dry.

Clean the whole skirted fleece, one batch at a time. Do not take any shortcuts. When your fleece is dry, card it very thoroughly and pluck out short bits, lumps, and scraps of grass or seeds. When the wool is very clean and well carded, the spinning will go easily.

Now it's time to spin. The most important question at this point is, "How thick?" Your machine's favorite yarn has a specific thickness. It may be called 2/4, 2/6, or 2/8. Take a piece of yarn that works well, and pick it apart so you can see a ply. Pull that ply tight between your fingers, and spin a yarn that looks exactly that thick. Practice until you can make such a yarn without producing lumps or breaks.

When you've got a few bobbins full of singles, make a two-ply yarn. Ply Z-twist if you've spun S-twist, and vice versa. Balance the twist of your plying against the twist of your spinning, so the two singles are well joined but not kinked together. A slightly unbalanced ply will skew the knitted stitches to one side. A very unbalanced ply will tweak into loops as the yarn enters the carriage, will jam in the needles (producing a break in the yarn), and will cause your fabric to drop onto the floor.

How much yarn is enough? How much did you use in your last few sweaters? How many balls did you go through, and how many yards were there in each ball? Multiply that one through. I allow about 2000 yards of two-ply per sweater, and spin half again as much as I think I'll need. Then I can set aside the thinnest and thickest skeins to make caps and mittens. I've also got them in reserve in case of emergency.

When you've spun and plied your yarn, measure it by winding skeins on a niddy noddy, on an umbrella swift marked for a two-yard circumference, or around the backs of chairs set to produce a one-, two-, or three-yard loop. Rinse the skeins in warm water and hang them up to dry.

When all the skeins are dry, inspect them. They should look like your millspun yarn, but glossier, stronger, and softer—as if they had the breath of life in them. Knit a sample swatch. Does it work? Knit two more little swatches, with lighter and looser tension. Take the swatches to the sink and full them, using warm water, and let them dry. Press them with a warm iron. All three should look very good, but one should have the tension just right.

Make a full-size gauge swatch, big enough to be really accurate. Full, dry, and press the swatch, then measure the whole thing and divide the number of stitches and the number of rows by inches. If all your yarn is the same thickness, go ahead and draft your sweater!

Knit more slowly than you usually do, so you can catch any mistakes before they happen.

All the care you've invested will be repaid with a truly wonderful garment.

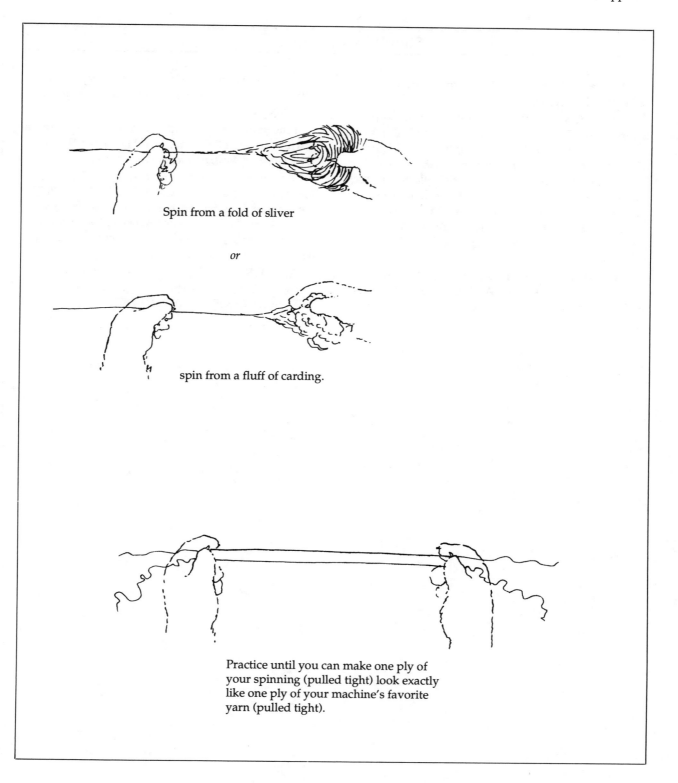

Spin from a fold of sliver

or

spin from a fluff of carding.

Practice until you can make one ply of
your spinning (pulled tight) look exactly
like one ply of your machine's favorite
yarn (pulled tight).

Suppliers and resources

These are my favorites. Find your own, but look for equivalent reliability.

Sportweight and other wool yarns from Jagger-Spun, Water Street, Springvale, ME 04083. (207) 324-4455. *JaggerSpun is an outstanding yarn company. They make superb yarns for knitting machines, and have wonderful colors. The yarns are simple and of excellent quality. Look for Jaggerspun in your local yarn shop. If they don't have it, make pleading noises until they do. If your retailer is unable to satisfy you, contact the company directly. These are good folks, and they'll help you.*

Cotton from Crystal Palace Yarns, 3006 San Pablo Avenue, Berkeley, CA 94702. *Crystal Palace is a wholesale supplier; look—or ask them—for a local retail dealer. The yarns are always good quality, and the staff are good folks. "Baby Georgia" is a superbly sensible cotton yarn.*

Handmade pewter buttons from Three Feathers Pewter, P.O. Box 232, Shreve, OH 44676. (216) 567-2047. *Good buttons, people, prices, service.*

Compuknit 910 from Knitking, 1128 Crenshaw Boulevard, Los Angeles, CA 90019. (213) 938-2077. *I've had four Knitking machines. They wear like Sherman tanks, and when they do need help, the service department is prompt and helpful. I expect my next four machines will also be Knitkings.*

Custom Knitting by Catherine Cartwright-Jones, c/o Interweave Press, 201 East Fourth Street, Loveland, CO 80537. (303) 669-7672.

Designer's Notebook

Inspiration!

Encouragement!

Charts!

You, too, can be a creative knitter. . . .

English-style Vest

- *English-style vest basics (pp. 97–105)*
- *V-neckline finish (pp. 37–39)*

FLOWERING VINE →

Technical notes: The crewneck pullover on page 204 was made of Demi-Georgia by Crystal Palace. The vest on page 194, the cape on page 201, and the coat on page 206 were made of yarn by Condon, which is no longer available, but could be made in Jaggerspun's heather yarns. The remaining garments are all made of Jaggerspun yarn.

All of the buttons were made by Three Feathers Pewter.

You may be able to make photocopy enlargements of the charts and trace them directly onto a grid for your machine. Try a 177% enlargement (for Knit-king/Brother 910 or 950; for 930 or 940, you can read the patterns in by disk); adjust by small increments until the grid corresponds to your pattern sheet. The smaller patterns will work on "punch-your-own-card" and bulky models.

The designs presented here are for individual inspiration and for personal use only. They may not be reproduced for commercial purposes without the author's permission. The photographs of the garments on pages 194 and 201 and of the gloves on page 200 are by Catherine Cartwright-Jones. All other photographs are by Joe Coca.

Drop-Shoulder Pullover

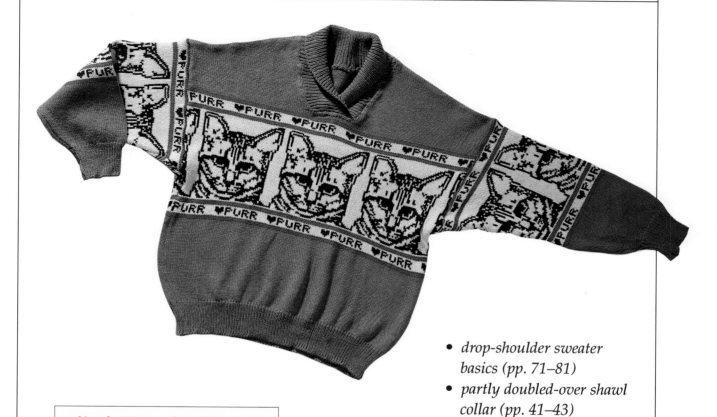

- *drop-shoulder sweater basics (pp. 71–81)*
- *partly doubled-over shawl collar (pp. 41–43)*

Your knitting machine, then, is a tabletop fabric shop, allowing you to make knitted fabric in just the colors, sizes, and patterns you love, ready for you to finish and sew up. This book stresses getting the fabric-making done quickly, because garments should be on people's backs, not in half-finished and long-procrastinated heaps. Perhaps you are blossoming with ideas for garments, and ready to fill everyone's closets, or perhaps you're stuck. If you need a spark, these pages contain some thoughts to get you going.

GRINNING TABBY

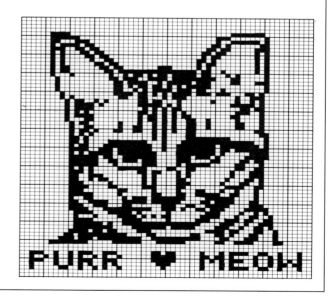

- drop-shoulder sweater basics (pp. 71–81)
- child's sweater (pp. 139–41)
- cardigan band (pp. 46–51)

SAINT AND DRAGON

TRIANGLE BORDER

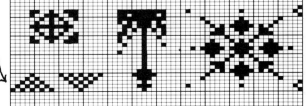

- *drop-shoulder sweater basics (pp. 71–81)*
- *crewneck finish (pp. 31–36)*
- *beret (pp. 157–59)*
- *gloves (pp. 170–79)*

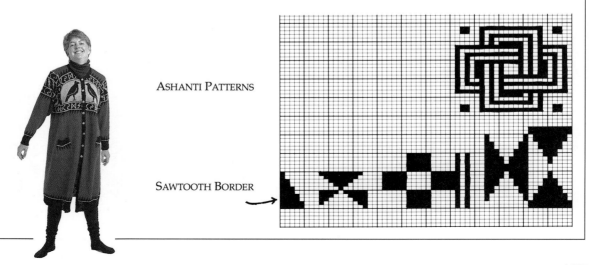

ASHANTI PATTERNS

SAWTOOTH BORDER

Raglan Cardigan

- *raglan sweater basics (pp. 83–95)*
- *cardigan band (pp. 46–51)*

You can see that the patterns vary between the two sleeves. What you can't see is that the back of this sweater is different than the front! The relationship between "ground" and "sky" is the same, but the bands of flowers and animals are different.

To make the clouds fade out in a natural way, I pushed the B-position needles (cloud) back to A position (sky) randomly on each row, through one repeat of the clouds.

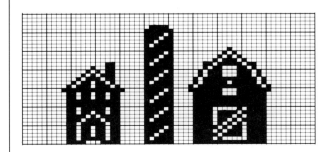

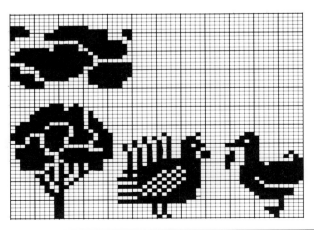

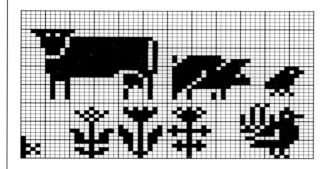

Make your own notebook; include anything that gets your circuits humming.

I added touches of embroidery throughout this sweater. The farmhouse and barn were decorated with duplicate stitch. The birds are long stitches, tacked down at their centers. The apples are big french knots.

199

Don't wait around for inspiration. Get to work making things, and ideas will come as your hands move. You cook three meals a day. All of your meals are edible, and some of them are terrific. If you waited around for culinary inspiration to strike, you'd starve before anything landed in the skillet. You get ideas for dinner once you start digging in the fridge, and ingredients tend to present themselves fortuitously. When you knit, start with some good-looking yarns, some measurements, and a few good notions, and see what bubbles up out of your subconscious stewpot.

- *cap (pp. 152–69)*
- *mittens and gloves (pp. 161–79)*

CLASSIC CAT
FAT CAT NAP
SNOWFLAKE

SMALL STAG on page 194.
HEART and PURR on page 195.

Hooded Cape

- *cape basics (pp. 107–113)*
- *hood (pp. 58–61)*

The seams in this cape have been accented with embroidered flowers and then laced together.

FLOWERING VINE and additional animal patterns on page 194.

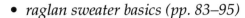

- *raglan sweater basics (pp. 83–95)*
- *English-style vest basics (pp. 97–105)*
- *child's sweater (pp. 139–41)*

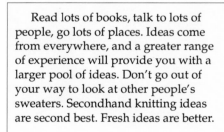

Read lots of books, talk to lots of people, go lots of places. Ideas come from everywhere, and a greater range of experience will provide you with a larger pool of ideas. Don't go out of your way to look at other people's sweaters. Secondhand knitting ideas are second best. Fresh ideas are better.

BLACK CAT

MEOW and PURR on page 195.
FAT CAT NAP on page 200

← At the edges of some patterns containing vertical lines, the stitches sometimes shift out of alignment. This happens most often when I am working with fine or slippery yarn. I whipstitch adjoining stitches together on the back to secure them.

↙ The edge stitches here have also been whipped together with sewing thread. In addition, the long floating yarns have been tacked down so they won't be snagged as the sweater is pulled on and off.

↘ The cat's yellow eyes were added in duplicate stitch.

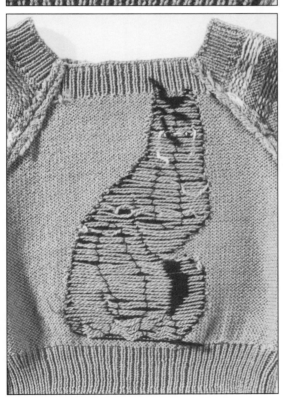

Drop-Shoulder Pullover with Bands

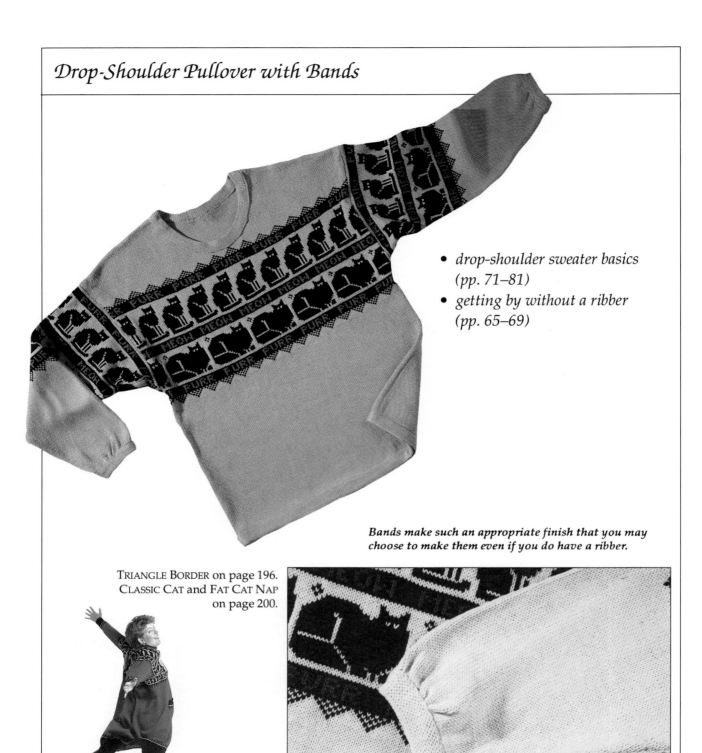

- *drop-shoulder sweater basics (pp. 71–81)*
- *getting by without a ribber (pp. 65–69)*

Bands make such an appropriate finish that you may choose to make them even if you do have a ribber.

TRIANGLE BORDER on page 196. CLASSIC CAT and FAT CAT NAP on page 200.

Drop-Shoulder Pullover and Closed-Finger Glove

- *drop-shoulder sweater basics (pp. 71–81)*
- *fully doubled-over shawl collar (pp. 40–43)*
- *gloves (pp. 170–79)*

CAT'S BREAKFAST
TABBY

When you are out of ideas, find ways to get them stirring again. If my pipeline to the unconscious is blocked, I go for a walk and do my version of a Navajo ceremonial chant, until the world is magnificent and vibrating like it was when I was four years old. I didn't learn the chant from the Navajo; I read it in *Krazy Kat*. [1] When I do it, I walk along and say to myself, *Beauty walks before me; beauty walks behind me; beauty is at my left; beauty is at my right; beauty is above me; beauty is below me; I walk in beauty.*

I visualize beauty as white light surrounding me: above me, below me, around me, and through me. After a mile or two, I feel like I'm cruising several feet above the ground and I'm ready to work. Invent your own tune-up!

---

[1] McDonnell, Patrick, Karen O'Connell, and Georgia Riley de Havenon. *Krazy Kat: The Comic Art of George Harriman*. New York: Abrams, 1986.

Coat

- *coat basics (pp. 115–125)*

Coat with Pockets

- coat basics
  (pp. 115–125)
- pockets (p. 64)

**The pockets complement
the coat's design in both
coloring and shape.**

RAVEN
RUNES
LIGHTNING

Index